FROM
PANIC
TO
PROFIT ®

HOW **6 KEY NUMBERS**® CAN MAKE A **6-FIGURE DIFFERENCE** IN YOUR **LAW FIRM**

FROM PANIC

TO PROFIT®

HOW **6 KEY NUMBERS**® CAN MAKE A **6-FIGURE DIFFERENCE** IN YOUR **LAW FIRM**

BROOKE E. LIVELY

Niche Pressworks

Indianapolis

FROM PANIC TO PROFIT®: How 6 Key Numbers® Can Make a 6-Figure Difference in Your Law Firm

ISBN 978-1-946533-76-0 E Book

    978-1-946533-90-6 Hardback

For permission to reprint portions of this content or bulk purchases, contact brooke@cathcap.com.

Published by Niche Pressworks, Indianapolis, IN

http://NichePressworks.com

Printed in the United States of America

CONTENTS

FOREWORD

On February 21, 2014 I walked away from a deal on ABC's *Shark Tank*. I went in asking for 200K for 5% of my company, DDPYOGA, Inc. They offered me 200K for 50% of my company. I knew that the program I had created was worth more than 400K. The Sharks had their concerns. "The fitness industry was too competitive," "You have peaked in profits," "Your profits are going to fall soon." I didn't let that slow me down, because I am unstoppable!

I never stop giving 100% for the things I believe in. I didn't let the fact that I couldn't read until I was 30 stop me. I didn't let the fact that I was 35 stop me from having one of the greatest wrestling careers of all time. I didn't let a potentially career ending injury to my L4 and L5 discs stop me from going on to become a Three Time World Wrestling Champion and Hall of Famer for the WWE. Instead, that injury spurred on the creation and development of my DDPY fitness program, the start of DDPYOGA and my appearance on *Shark Tank*.

The week following my segment on *Shark Tank*, our sales broke $1,000,000! Our sales continued to grow at an exponential rate. We were hitting new goals and blasting through our expectations. We started to develop a smartphone app, *DDPYOGANow*, and knew that this was a major piece to our success. We had money rolling in and needed to increase staff, production, and management. We were a young company and had many things to learn. While we knew the basics of our financial numbers and were manually keeping track of our sales, we also knew that we needed help in learning how to streamline, automate and improve these processes to continue to grow as a company. Internally we disagreed about how to move forward with accurate reporting and financial analysis. We decided that we needed a team of knowledgeable, dedicated, and hard-working professionals to get us to where we wanted to be. That's when we hired Cathedral Capital to elevate our financial understanding, automate our systems and bring us up to date on our financial practices. And they delivered!

I have been an entrepreneur all my life. I have always known that being knowledgeable about your finances was important. I am fiscally conservative and don't believe in debt. I always want to have enough cash flow to get me through any unforeseen events. When I saw that we were a rapidly growing business and that our numbers continued to escalate, I realized we needed the help.

What a difference a year makes! Because of the efforts of the team at Cathedral Capital, I now get accurate financial reports, daily sales, budgets, and where we are in monthly goals emailed to me every day. I have our financials right at my fingertips. Because of Cathedral Capital, we have fixed our financial disagreements within our company and have made positive changes to continue the growth of DDPY! I have a plan for the next year and we are on track for where we thought we would be. I am now confident in my financial planning for the years to come. This renewed confidence gives me the ability to continually move forward and reach more people about a healthier, more positive life!

I am a teacher who believes that healthy living is the best thing you can do for yourself. When Brooke asked me to write a forward to help her spread her message of fiscal health, I immediately agreed. I am a believer that you must always keep learning to keep growing. My financial team and I have benefited so much from Brooke's knowledge. I am unstoppable! Brooke is unstoppable! And, thanks to the hard work put in by Cathedral Capital and knowledge passed on through Brooke and her team, DDPY is unstoppable!

Remember, if you believe you can, or you believe you can't, you're right! BANG!

Diamond Dallas Page

Owner and CEO of DDPYOGA, Inc.

You can find more information about *Positively Unstoppable,* the DDPY program, and our smartphone app, *DDPYNow,* on our website www.ddpyoga.com

A SUCCESSFUL FIRM IS A JOURNEY

It is not the mountain we conquer but ourselves.

— SIR EDMUND HILLARY

I love this quote for many reasons. One is that the author of the quote, Sir Edmund Hillary, was the first person to scale Mount Everest. The other reason is the analogy between climbing and pursuing your passion. I'm not a mountain climber, but I do have a passion for hiking—so much so that when coming up with a logo for my company, I chose to make a mountain central to the image. I love the idea of conquering the challenges and peaks ahead.

This quote came to life for me in a very real way a few years ago as I was making a career transition and about to launch Cathedral Capital. I went on a hike with a friend. It was supposed to be a "Moderate to Advanced" hike, but to be honest, it kicked my butt. Looking back, I just wasn't prepared for the physical and mental challenges. There were several things I underestimated about how that day would go, and one thing I definitely didn't plan on was not being able to reach the top.

In my head, I began that day believing I was going to reach that mountain top. But I didn't make it. And let's be clear, I TRIED to keep pushing onward and upward, keeping my eye on the goal. But I reached a point where I just knew it wasn't going to happen ... at least not that day. The mountain completely humbled me. However, as with any "failure to achieve your mission," I also learned several lessons. Those lessons have been instrumental to me while building my business.

First, always have a vision plan. The key word there being "plan," because a vision only has value when there's a clear plan for execution. Combining your vision with a plan makes it far more likely that you'll achieve it.

Second, you need a Sherpa. To reach the top of Mount Everest, Sir Edmund Hillary traveled with a Sherpa by the name of Tenzing Norgay, who guided him every step of the way. Tenzing's job was to help execute the plan (by staying on top of a million details and having a ton of experience) that would allow Sir Edmund Hillary to achieve his vision of being the first person to reach the top of Mount Everest. I could have really used a Sherpa that day.

The idea of a Sherpa cemented in my eyes the value we provide clients. Cathedral Capital is a Sherpa for its clients. We provide strategic and logistical support to help entrepreneurs achieve their goals.

Let me tell you something else about that mountain. I went back. And this time, I went with my sister, who is highly experienced and knew the trail. She could tell me what possible dangers lay ahead, and she also helped me set a realistic pace to finish. And even though my sister had to verbally and physically pull and push me to the top, I made it.

That mountain, Cathedral Lake, became my company's logo because of what it represents in my life. Like the quote says, it was less about conquering the mountain, it was about conquering a goal I set for myself. That mountain made me realize that you can accomplish anything you put your mind to as long as you have an actionable vision plan and a Sherpa.

I like to think of my company, Cathedral Capital, as a financial Sherpa. I'm passionate about numbers. I'm passionate about building leaders. And I'm passionate about finding where these intersect for entrepreneurs and small business owners. My greatest joy comes from walking alongside my clients—helping them chart their course, overcome obstacles, discover their hidden strengths, and scale the peaks they never imagined they could conquer.

Let's start your climb.

– **Brooke**

INTRODUCTION

I talk to a lot of attorneys. A LOT. And most of them even feel comfortable enough to share with me what is really happening in their practice. How do we get to this point?

I tell them the truth. And the truth is—I'VE SEEN WORSE.

I promise you; I have seen worse. I have seen people carrying over six figures of credit card debt (yes, take a moment and do that math). I have talked to people who owe the IRS more than one million dollars in payroll taxes. I have worked with attorneys whose whole dysfunctional family worked in the firm, and some were stealing. I have seen more firms than I ever thought I would who didn't have "books." They literally looked at the bank balance to see if they could write a check or process payroll.

Here is another thing I consistently see. Lawyers who made the best decision they could at the time. They worked hard and made the math work—even if it meant that they made some less than desirable moves. They racked up credit card debt; they raided their retirement accounts; they maxed out their lines of credit; they borrowed from their credit card processing company; they sold flat fee work that wouldn't be done for months and used the money to pay rent that day. But they kept their firm alive. They kept food on their tables and the tables of their employees. They laid awake at night, worrying about how (and if) it was going to work out. They did what it took.

And then one day, they gathered enough courage to call me and ask for help. I'm going to tell you a lot of their stories over the

1

next few chapters. These are the people who didn't want to live with all the stress, chaos, embarrassment, and isolation they were feeling. They wanted to live a more "profitable" life. And they are the heroes of this book.

CHAPTER 1

6 KEY NUMBERS® THAT CAN CHANGE YOUR LIFE

"Imagine you are vacationing at a beautiful island resort with no phones or internet, and the only contact with the outside world is by way of a supply boat that comes once a week. What three pieces of information from the office do you need to know to decide if you can stay another week?" Wow.

Somebody asked me this question in a meeting one day. I was overwhelmed. Surely, I needed more than three pieces of information? Did I want information about my cash? My people? What about the sales process? And within those categories, what actual one piece of information would I need? And which ones would give me an accurate enough idea of what was going on to allow me to make a decision about staying in paradise for another week?

Over the next few years, my team and I started answering these questions for ourselves and for our clients. We found that there are six areas that have critically important information—the type of info you need when you are sitting at a fabulous island resort. And while all firms are different, we know there is one Key Number in each section that applies to your firm. The Key Number is almost always forward-looking—meaning it tells you what is going to happen. And when it isn't forward-looking, it tells you how to get back on track.

As with many things, our answer to this question changed over the years. By working with a variety of firms, we learned about more practice areas in more parts of the country than we ever thought possible. My team and I used trial and error to develop new numbers and scrapped the ones that didn't get us the information we wanted. We eliminated some numbers once we figured out that they were the building blocks for the number that actually mattered. After six years and more than 100 law firms, we believe we finally have the answers that let us spend another week in paradise.

When most of our clients come to us, they aren't spending weeks at a time on a remote island; they are working hard, trying to keep their firm afloat. Patricia is a great example of that. She owns a law firm with revenues of $750K last year. Her client billings allow her to keep up the appearance of prosperity even though she lies awake at night worrying about money. She is tech-savvy and uses an app on her phone to track the cash she has in the bank.

Patricia wants to grow her firm and feels confident in her ability to do this using the tens of thousands of dollars owed to her in Accounts Receivable. Her revenue is unpredictable, which makes her react to whatever crisis is the loudest or most dire, and she finds herself constantly putting out fires. Patricia feels like she worries about cash all the time, but especially the first and third weeks of the month when rent and payroll checks get cut.

Patricia has a nagging feeling that she might be missing something. What makes things worse is that she isn't sure if the "something" means her business can't achieve her long-term vision, or even scarier, if the "something" simply means her business isn't sustainable.

Many attorneys can readily identify with Patricia. They understand the stress, the not knowing what the next move should be, and the insecurity that comes along with all of that. In addition, they are attorneys who should always "know" the answers. When you are supposed to have all the answers, who can you turn to in this situation?

Patricia turned to our company, Cathedral Capital, and we immediately sprang into action. What we discovered is that it doesn't matter if you are sitting on an island or struggling to keep your firm going, the 6 Key Numbers that you need to know are the same. These numbers help you gain control, chart a path, and achieve your goals.

Each of the 6 Key Numbers falls into its own category. As we go through the book, I'll explain the category, point out the Key Number, and tell you how to use it effectively. Here's a quick preview:

Category	Components	Key Number
Cash	Cash Balance A/R Monthly Nut	Cash Flow Forecast
Ideal Ratios	Rule of Thirds Payroll Marketing Overhead	Owner Compensation
Production	Capacity Utilization Billing Goals	WIP (Work in Progress)
Budget vs. Actual	Profit Plan Billing Grid	Budget vs. Actual
Marketing and Sales	Conversion Cycle Conversion Rates by Referral Source	Sales Calls Booked
Case Management	Average Price Average Length Average Staffing	Net New Cases

Cash

Cash is king, and no firm can survive without an ample amount. More than anything else, you need to know about the cash you have—and the cash you are about to need. Starting with your true cash balance and adding Accounts Receivable (A/R) and your monthly "nut" (the approximate amount it costs to run your firm for a month), you arrive at a Cash Flow Forecast. Your CFF allows you to look forward, make decisions, and plan in a measured, reasoned, and proactive way, instead of reacting to a new crisis every week.

Key Number – Cash Flow Forecast

Ideal Ratios

The question we are asked most often is, "How much should I be spending on … " The good news is that we have the answer. We use a ratio to determine what's called the Rule of Thirds. We'll get into the details later, but it is important to know these ratios and how they can help you focus both time and money. Most importantly, you need to ensure *you are getting paid*. The old axiom of "pay yourself first" is true, though we call it planning for profit. Law firm owners work much too hard to be the last ones to be paid. You are taking the risk and should be reaping the financial reward. For this reason, we always monitor the owner benefit—and look for opportunities to increase it.

Key Number – Owner Compensation

Production

At the end of the day, if your law firm is not producing legal services, it will close. The trick is to learn how to incentivize your people through goal-setting and understand what the capacity of the firm is and how much of that capacity you are using. WIP (Work in Progress) is the key number for production. Today's WIP is next month's revenue.

Key Number - WIP

Budget vs. Actual

The Budget vs. Actual report is a standard report in all accounting software and serves two purposes. First, it means you have a budget. We don't like the word budget because it implies limitations, so we prefer to call them Profit Plans (because who doesn't want more profit?). This is an opportunity to dream, to plan, to start to create the firm of your dreams. The Budget vs. Actual report lets you know if you are straying off course and gives you the ability to course correct.

Key Number – Budget vs. Actual Report

Marketing and Sales

Understanding how clients get to you is vital. Once you start tracking your conversion cycle, it highlights places in marketing where your message is not in alignment with your firm. It also gives you concrete numbers about what happens once a potential client starts the sales process. Ultimately, the Key Number we track is the number of Sales Calls Booked. With that one number, we can predict how many new cases will be signed in the next month.

Key Number – Sales Calls Booked

Case Management

I have met a lot of attorneys in my life (my father, my brother, two uncles, too many cousins to count, and virtually every man I ever dated, plus all our clients over the years), so I know your reaction to what I am about to say next. I realize no case is "normal," but your cases do have certain similar characteristics. Your average case length and value tell us a lot about what is going to happen in your firm when paired with the Net New Cases key number. By knowing the number of Net New Cases (cases opened minus cases closed), we can predict how much work is in the firm, the pressure it will put on your team, and next month's revenue.

Key Number – Net New Cases

Each of the 6 Key Numbers provides insight into the financial health of your firm. They are also the basic numbers that successful firms use to track where they are to make sure they are on a path to profitability. None of the numbers are hard to find. None are difficult to understand. Throughout the book, we'll examine each of the 6 Key Numbers in greater detail, providing examples, tips, and stories to help you better understand and apply each one to your firm. Each one can be implemented individually to put you on the path to clarity (and profitability). Together, they are a powerful tool to help you create the firm of your dreams.

But let's get back to Patricia so you can see an example of the 6 Key Numbers at work. We started with cash. The first thing we did was take away the bank app on her phone and teach her how to find her real cash balance. A better understanding of where she stood helped give her a greater sense of security about her financial stability. We then looked at her Accounts Receivable and implemented some simple but powerful tools to raise her collection rate. This meant she had more cash in the bank. Those first and third weeks, when payroll and rent had to be paid, were no longer quite as scary. We also looked at how much she needed to get through the month—her monthly "nut."

> Each of the 6 Key Numbers® provides insight into the financial health of your firm.

It was time to implement the first Key Number—Cash Flow Forecast. We taught her how to predict how much cash she would have on hand at the end of every week, for the next six to eight weeks. With this information, she could finally breathe.

After dealing with cash at the office, we wanted to look at the cash she was taking home. The second category we addressed was her ratios—what was happening to her revenue. By analyzing the ratios on her P&L (Profit and Loss), we determined that she was not receiving very much financial benefit from her firm. All the money that should have been in Patricia's pocket was going to her staff and to overspending on marketing. By creating new compensation packages for her team and making better decisions about how she spent her marketing dollars, Patricia increased her owner benefit. Now, not only was she not worrying about money at the office, she wasn't worrying about money at home.

The next step was to look at the productivity of her team. We set billing goals and held her team accountable. Once we knew how much capacity she had and saw how much her team was producing, we began to understand whether or not her team was overloaded. At this point, Patricia started to feel as if she was working proactively since hiring decisions could be made in advance, not simply when her team told her they were overloaded and overworked. But the number she liked best was the WIP report she received at the end of each week. Using that, she knew exactly when the team had worked enough to cover next month's "nut." And nothing was better than knowing that every hour billed after that was gravy—cash in her pocket.

Working with Patricia, we knew she had some long-term goals that she wanted to meet. In order to achieve those goals, she needed a budget, or as we like to call it, a Profit Plan. The Profit Plan set financial parameters and guideposts for Patricia. After that was in place, we moved to the final stage—setting up a system where she could compare her Profit Plan to what actually happened every month. Now, she not only had a plan, but she had a way to see if she was on track or not. Patricia could quickly identify where she needed to make adjustments, what worked, and what needed to be changed or revised. She started to check goals off her list.

At some point in the life of your firm, you realize that you want to be able to control the flow of new clients and understand how your marketing affects that flow. Because Patricia had the basic numbers down, she was ready to take a more proactive approach to acquiring new clients. We helped her track every potential client from first contact to signed engagement letter. We knew where they came from and what marketing had brought them to us. The conversion cycle showed Patricia what worked and what didn't in her marketing. It also showed her what changes or training were needed to keep potential clients moving through her pipeline. Once she understood this, one simple number—Sales Calls Booked—told her how many new clients would come on board in the next month.

Knowing the number of new cases is great, but as Cuba Gooding, Jr. says in *Jerry Maguire*, "SHOW ME THE MONEY!" Gathering some easy information from Patricia's firm management software enabled us to learn about her average case. Once we knew the average length and value, we could predict revenues in the coming months and how that would affect her team's workload. The number that mattered to Patricia was Net New Cases (cases opened minus cases closed). Using that number, she could see what would happen over the next few months.

Cathedral Capital's 6 Key Numbers transformed Patricia's business. Instead of constantly worrying about finances, she has a plan in place to continuously monitor and manage her funds and profitability. She now sleeps soundly, knowing where she stands financially and what is going to happen in the future. These 6 Key Numbers allow for faster and easier decisions. Patricia is now in a position to make a decision about extending her fabulous island vacation.

Our approach takes information you already have or can easily obtain and organizes it into a powerful structure that allows you to better access and marshal your resources and capabilities. While Patricia is a composite created from the hundreds of attorneys I have met and worked with over the years, her story embodies the types of challenges and worries faced by many law firms. Rest assured, you are not alone. Change for the better is possible if you know what to look for and how to create a plan.

Remember my attempt to reach Cathedral Lake? As you read this book, think of the numbers I share as a trail map to help you get to the top of *your* mountain. At the end of each chapter, you will see a section summarizing what the "Number" is, what it tells you, and how often you should look at it. At the very bottom, you get to give yourself a grade. This will help you determine if you have a good trail map or if you need to hire a better Sherpa.

Change for the better is possible if you know what to look for and how to create a plan

CHAPTER 2

CASH IS KING

There is nothing more important to a business than cash. Because of this, it is also the piece of a business that creates the most stress for owners—and law firms are no exception. Cash numbers build upon and connect to each other. It starts with your true cash balance, adds in accounts receivables and anticipated revenue, then subtracts out anticipated expenses. The result gives you a week-by-week map of how much cash you are going to have. It lets you know if there is a problem headed your way and gives you time to react. With this, you can make a measured decision in advance, rather than a quick choice in panic mode.

Understanding Your Balance

Strictly speaking, a cash balance is the total amount of money you have in an account, including deposits and all expenditures (pending and actual). It is the foundation upon which all other numbers rest. Until you know where you stand, you can't make any decisions or moves. It is also the number that keeps many of our new clients awake at night. For these two reasons, we always start by understanding your cash balance.

When running a business, it's important to know what funds you have available. You know that really handy app you have on your phone where you can pull up your bank balance? Well, I have news—that is not your cash balance. Here's why.

That number does not take into account any checks you or your bookkeeper may have written or any electronic payments that have not cleared (like payroll, payroll taxes, or credit card payments). It also doesn't track recent credit card payments that typically take one or two days to get deposited in your account. A good accounting software program can solve these information gaps.

The elusiveness of knowing your cash balance reminds me of a sales call I had a few years ago with Robert and his partners.[1] At one of our first meetings, Robert kept talking about not knowing how much cash they had available, and at that moment, I realized they didn't use any accounting software. Whenever they needed to write a check or process payroll, Robert went around the office with the bank's phone app, asking the other three partners if they had

Understanding "The Float"

Understanding your cash balance requires an understanding of "the float." It's a concept that many business owners don't completely understand (or are not even aware of). Others "survive" on the float— basically hoping things won't clear before they can make a deposit. (This is also known as check kiting or fraud.)

Essentially, the float refers to the lag time between when you write a check and when the money actually leaves your account.

Just because the money hasn't left your account doesn't mean that it's available to spend. Your true cash balance is what you have available after taking the float into account.

---

[1] Robert is not his real name. No real names have been used in this book. However, since I need to call people something, I am using names from my family. Good thing I have a BIG family. Robert is a very entrepreneurial cousin. After working for a few years, he looked for a company to buy. He now manufactures skylights.

written any checks that hadn't cleared. This firm had a lot of moving parts—23 people on payroll, with millions of dollars in billings each year. That is a lot of information to keep in your head. And they couldn't.

Invariably, one of the partners would write a check and then boom—something would clear that they forgot about. It was a stressful way to run a company—and live. The first thing I did was hire them a bookkeeper. It was about six months before they were ready to work with us. But when Robert and his partners did come on, they told us how much better they felt now that they knew their true cash balance.

And where did they find this number? In QuickBooks. QuickBooks works just like that old check register you used to have to balance every month—back in the old days before bank apps were available. QuickBooks keeps an accurate record of all the money that moves through your firm. It is where you can find out *exactly* how much money you have at any given time.

Let's look at an example of how checking the bank app instead of your true cash balance in your bookkeeping program can backfire because of the float.

Say you check your business account on your phone, and you have $12,000 available. You write an $8,000 check to a court reporter, assuming you'll have $4,000 in cash left over afterward. But then, a $6,000 check you wrote to rent last week suddenly clears (thank you, float!). The court reporter's check then bounces; he gets mad and refuses to show up today for the deposition. All of a sudden, you're racing to put out fire after fire.

Accounting software programs take this into consideration, so what you see is what you get—a real-time understanding of your cash balance.

It may be tough to break the habit of checking your current bank balance before making payments, especially if you are a younger person who has never been exposed to the idea of a check register, or if you're really tight on cash. However, it's vitally important to be mindful of your actual cash balance before making payments.

A final note—your cash balance is the foundation for all other numbers in your practice. You should look at this number once a week, or more if you have been using an app and are trying to get in the habit of checking your "true" cash balance.

Automating Your Balance

Bookkeeping is no longer a manual job. With the advent of electronic financial management, it's not necessary to track checks and credit card payments manually.

By far, the most prevalent bookkeeping program for small law firms is Intuit's QuickBooks. Intuit is, and has been, the industry leader for many years. Its functionality is incredible. We often have clients who come to us saying they want a fully integrated solution. I understand this, having made that decision myself when I was running a firm. Even though attorneys have to do a little finagling when it comes to IOLTA accounting, QuickBooks Online is still our first choice. And once you have QuickBooks, you can set up "feeds" that automatically record all transactions with your bank and all your credit cards. How easy is that?

The next step is figuring out the best practice management software for your company. Options are becoming more and more sophisticated, and many have accounting features built in. We found that software with built-in accounting features is generally not the best solution. The software is designed for timekeeping, document creation and storage, and keeping track of deadlines. As a consequence, the accounting module often ends up having limited functionality, almost as if bolted on as an afterthought.

Different practice management offerings sync with QuickBooks, but syncing is a manual process and not always reliable. Fortunately, more options that seamlessly integrate with QuickBooks are coming on the market. This is a much better situation.

Practice Panther is a great example of a software option that fully integrates with QuickBooks. Imagine doing everything from logging time, running bills, and even recording deposits and writing checks right from your practice management software—and it all magically shows up in QuickBooks!

Accounts Receivable

Accounts Receivable (A/R) is money you already earned. You billed for the completed work, but clients have yet to pay. Simply put, it is the time between when you bill clients and when they pay you. Even more simply put, it is the difference between being very profitable and just barely hanging on.

Because of this difference (and its importance), Accounts Receivable is the second number we need to get under control. We are pretty passionate about this topic because businesses can't survive (let alone thrive) unless they successfully collect the money they are owed. Since it is essential to have a clear understanding of how this piece of your business works, let's get back to basics.

What is A/R? Most people would say it is when somebody doesn't pay you. True, but it goes deeper than that. Think of it like this. You have provided a service that cost you time and money. Until you're paid, you basically gave a loan to a client at zero percent interest—out of your very own pocket. And what's worse, it is an unsecured loan!

If a client doesn't pay you for your time and money, you can't go to the phone company and explain that you can't pay your bill because Joe Schmoe hasn't paid yet, but he should pay soon, so don't worry. I'm also pretty certain that your attorneys and paralegals won't appreciate a delayed payroll run because you're waiting on Joe Schmoe's money.

It just doesn't work that way. You still need to run a firm, meaning pay bills, make payroll, and continue conducting business.

When you think of A/R as a loan, you should start to feel more proactive about collecting the money you are owed. As we go through this section, keep that in mind and use it as motivation to implement steps and to create systems that ensure you're compensated for your work.

Aging A/R

Running an Aging A/R report can tell you a lot about your business and your clients. Essentially, the report provides a snapshot of the company's accounts receivable process, organized into date ranges and how long invoices have been outstanding. With this information, you can identify clients who pay on time and those who do not.

To get the most accurate Aging A/R report, your bookkeeper should generate one using your practice management software. These reports look something like this:

	Current	1 - 30	31 - 60	61 - 90	91 and over	Total
Dewey Cheatum and Howe, LLC **A/R Aging Summary** As of September 30						
Anderson, Bartholomew			114.98			114.98
Anderson, Catherine			3,766.00			3,766.00
Bare, Catherine		300.00				300.00
Baxter, Roxanna					1,700.00	1,700.00
Birmingham, Thomas					98.75	98.75
Breadwell, Elizabeth		1,000.00				1,000.00
Brooks, Edwin		445.34				445.34
Bryan, Hannah		2,175.00				2,175.00
Cain, Harriet			4,710.00			4,710.00
Caine, John			6,120.00			6,120.00
Chapman, Joseph		2,187.50				2,187.50
Coppage, Jeremiah		862.50	1,312.50			2,175.00
Dawson, Elizabeth Ann			540.00			540.00
Dawson, Sarah		1,400.55				1,400.55
Easley, Mamie			4,080.00			4,080.00
Hooe, Polly					860.32	860.32
Kelly, Fletcher					56.25	56.25
Kelly, Rowan			3,766.00			3,766.00
Morehead, Joseph	680.00					680.00
Nelson, Lydia			4,500.00			4,500.00
Noe, Martha Jane		981.25				981.25
Phoebe, Phelby			3,540.00		24,620.02	28,160.02
Presley, Turner			262.50		262.50	525.00
Quiggan, Robert					697.15	697.15
Scarborough, James					196.56	196.56
Shelley, J. D.		150.00				150.00
Stark, Barsheba			3,166.68			3,166.68
Talbert, Pearl			20.80			20.80
Tucker, Lorena		352.50				352.50
Turner, Elizabeth				4,080.00	.	4,080.00
Weir, Janetta		428.15	2,981.25			3,409.40
Whitson, Sarah					118.75	118.75
Wolf, Hannah			4,080.00			4,080.00
TOTAL	$ 680.00	$ 10,282.79	$ 38,880.71	$ 4,080.00	$ 28,610.30	$ 82,533.80

The left-hand side of the report lists client names. The columns show the amount owed by each client, broken down into specific time ranges: 0–30, 31–60, 61–90, and 91+ days. There are also totals at the bottom of each column, so you can see how much you are owed. An Aging A/R report provides a goldmine of information. You can find out easy things, like who owes you money, and more interesting things, like whether certain clients usually pay late. It's useful to know which clients pay on time, which ones consistently pay late, and which ones have stopped paying altogether. It may help you decide which case you start working on next.

As you look at the report, focus on clients who owe you money in multiple columns. That means not only do they owe you money from past bills, but that you're still doing work for them. If they aren't paying you and you're still working for them, you need to think about changing your methods. In these situations, we suggest our clients answer two questions:

- What are you doing to get the money collected?
- How do you plan to stop working on current cases for which you may or may not get paid?

Stop-Work Policy

We met an attorney from Oregon named Paige,[2] who had an ingenious solution for effectively and efficiently managing nonpaying clients. She implemented what she called the Red Rubber Band Policy. The beauty of her solution is its simplicity.

When a client owed the firm money for 90 days, Paige notified the client in writing and put a red rubber band on the file to stop work. Any attorney or paralegal who went to pull a file and found a red rubber band knew that file was off-limits. Paige and anybody else in the firm who saw a red rubber band file (or even just the red rubber band!) on somebody's desk would immediately ask why the person was working a file that had been cut off. The policy was understood and followed throughout the firm.

---

[2]   Paige is actually my first cousin once removed. She owns a PR agency.

Not every solution has to be high tech and expensive. In fact, many good solutions are available at your local office supply store.[3] Whether you use this method or another one, every firm should have a stop-work policy.[4]

> Not every solution has to be high tech and expensive

Generating Aging A/R reports simplifies the triggering of a stop-work policy. The numbers don't lie. It's easy to see who is paying and who is not paying. In this mix, it's also important to examine the clients who pay on time. Knowing which clients pay on time can help direct how you manage your practice going forward. You may decide to cultivate this client base by giving their work priority or additional focus. It's a positive outcome and can help make long-term planning decisions by helping you decide where to put more energy and what you may need to step away from.

Fixable Habits

When we start working with most firms, their collection rate is typically 70–80 percent. That reflects the national average for law firms,[5] and most firms just view it as how a business is run. In fact, we often hear the uncollected money referred to as "the cost of doing business." We know this is not the cost of doing business, and that it is a fixable problem. The solution involves looking at collections as two separate issues. First, the cost of collecting late and unpaid invoices involves money, time, and valuable resources. It can feel like a distraction from your work, and it probably is. This brings us to the second problem. If you don't effectively collect payment for your services, you're working for free. That is a big problem.

---

[3] "Big Bands" are about $2.50 a pack, available at Office Depot, and perfect for this task.

[4] Check your Bar rules, people. Every state is different.

[5] Legal Trends Report Powered by Clio 2019, Clio, Accessed October 25, 2019, https://2b9twj15256023uw4w1i3g6q-wpengine.netdna-ssl.com/wp-content/uploads/2019/10/2019-Legal-Trends-Report.pdf.

Cost of Collecting

Collecting payments comes with tangible costs. Most attorneys don't think a great deal about the effort required to collect that 70–80 percent. Somehow, since the number falls into the cost of doing business, it gets overlooked. But in many cases, it may mean sending multiple bills, waiting up to 90 days for payment, and even having a billing clerk, office manager, paralegal, or assigned attorney call the delinquent client. If it goes on for too long, the firm's owner often gets involved, either by making a call or sending a letter.

That's a lot of steps to take to ensure payment and reveals an often unnoticed opportunity cost to firms. Think of it this way. Just like when you are working a case, every time someone picks up that invoice to collect it, it costs you money. When someone at your firm is trying to collect money, it means they aren't picking up another client's file and billing. Each step in the collection process is time that could be spent on billable tasks.

The other cost of late collection is mental. Few people enjoy collecting money from clients who aren't paying. As a result, one of three things happen:

- They do it but are cranky around the office, which makes others cranky.
- They see how much A/R there is and wonder about the financial stability of the firm.
- They avoid collecting the money.

The first two impact the morale of your team and increase employee turnover. It takes an average of 36 days to fill an empty position, and when you add almost $15,000 in hiring costs plus more than a month in lost billing, that number is almost $60,000.[6,7] So low company morale can really add up. While collecting money can cost a lot, avoiding the collection process leads us straight to the second problem.

---

[6]   Assumes 120 billable hour goal per month at a rate of $350 per hour.

[7]   2017 Talent Acquisition Benchmarking Report, SHRM Society for Human Resources Management. Accessed October 25, 2019, https://www.shrm.org/hr-today/trends-and-forecasting/research-and-surveys/Documents/2017-Talent-Acquisition-Benchmarking.pdf.

Working for Free

In addition to the dilemmas encountered when collecting unpaid invoices, A/R presents unique challenges for firm owners. Some may see it as an unrecoverable loss that is too bothersome to recoup. Others take a different approach. They view A/R as an informal savings plan. It exists out there, and when they need it, they can ask for it. Neither of these approaches is terribly sound.

Here are a few fun A/R facts:

- Accounts Receivable are like rotting fruit; every day that goes by, they are worth less than the day before.

- After 90 days, on average, we believe only about 10 percent of A/R is collectable.

- A 75 percent collection rate is like a car dealership giving away every fourth car—for FREE.

Basically, the longer someone doesn't pay you, the less likely it is to happen. If you think that's demotivating, think about a 75 percent collection rate. It means that your firm is working the last week of every month for free. I guarantee that your team would much rather work three weeks and then go on vacation for that fourth week, as opposed to working for no reason. Most owners feel the same way, but since they have it in their mind that it is "the cost of doing business," most firms just live with it. They may look at the A/R report when feeling tight on cash and try to collect what they can, but the rest of the time, they do their best to ignore the money piling up (or, rather, not piling up).

> The longer someone doesn't pay you, the less likely it is to happen

Some firms view their A/R as a piggy bank. They earned the money and expect that when they really need it, they can call the clients who will (happily) pay them. You see the flaw with this reasoning, right? But these firms may double-down on that logic and explain that since the money hasn't been collected, they haven't had to pay income tax on it. These attorneys are right. You don't have to pay income tax on money you don't have, but that means you don't have the money! Also, a client who hasn't paid for 6–8 months is extremely unlikely to happily cough up cash just because you ask.

The way to mitigate these issues is by preventing A/R in the first place, and this is done the first day you meet a potential client. The medium is your Fee Agreement. By favorably rewriting your Fee Agreement, you can control when and how you get paid. Here are some best practices:

- Include a paragraph that addresses withdrawal for nonpayment.
- Get the first three months' worth of billing in the Initial Retainer.
- Set an Evergreen Retainer amount that is equal to an average of three months of billing.
- Accept credit cards.
- Take payment timing out of the clients' hands by automatically charging them after the bill is sent.

While this can entail a significant rewriting of your Fee Agreement, it is more than worth it.

For detailed information on how to rewrite your Fee Agreement, see the **How To** section at the end of the book.

Outcomes Don't Lie

So what happens when you make all the suggested revisions to your Fee Agreement? Nirvana! Just kidding, but it is pretty great. Almost all of our clients have collection rates of over 90 percent. That's 15 percent above where they were when they started with us. That is absolutely worth taking a three percent haircut on the credit card merchant service fees.

While 15 percent is a pretty abstract thing, $150,000 is not. Let me explain. We have a client in the Pacific Northwest named Katherine[8] who came to us with the typical 72 percent collection rate on just over $1 million in billing. We quickly raised her collection rate by 15 percent (up to 87 percent), which netted her an additional $150,000 the first year.

This cash was much appreciated since she had a son leaving for college soon. Think about that for a minute. In less than a year, without doing any additional work and by simply changing the way she approached her Fee Agreement and set expectations in the sales call, Katherine was able to pay almost three years of tuition.

The longer firms have these protections in place, the better they work. Invariably, after we put everything in position and more money starts to roll in every month, somebody in the firm gets lazy with either the Fee Agreement or making sure the evergreen replenishments are getting done. All of a sudden, cash starts to dry up. The owner of the firm is reminded again how important it is to keep these structures in place and what a huge difference they make. Consequently, they double down and get really serious about enforcing the Fee Agreement, both with clients and within the firm. This is when their collection rate soars past 90 percent.

Let's close this section with a brief story. I was recently talking to a client, Sam, in California about this chapter. When I told him I was going to talk about a 90 percent collection goal, he laughed and said that was way too low. He asked why I didn't tell the truth? He has a 98 percent collection rate. I told him nobody would believe me, and I would lose all credibility. I include this here because Sam was pretty passionate that I level with everybody who reads this book

---

[8]   This is my great-grandmother's name (and six or eight cousins).

that 90 percent is just a starting goal, and 95 percent plus is where you should be aiming. Thanks, Sam![9]

Your Fee Agreement is your weapon to combat A/R. It is the first, second, and third line of defense. It is the document that governs your relationship with your client, so it might as well help your business as much as it helps your client. We know we make it sound like a magic document, but really, it is.

Cash Flow Forecast

At the beginning of the book, we talk about the fact that we have a specific order for these numbers. We use them in this order because they build on each other—and the Cash Flow Forecast is the first place where you can really see how they work together.

Up until now, the reports we looked at have been backward facing, meaning they tell you what has happened—how much money is in the bank, and how much money clients owe us. Now, it is time to start looking forward.

Since you have a good idea of where you stand, we can start assembling information to see where you are going to be. Here is how it works. You take all the info we've collected so far:

- Cash Balance – how much money you are starting with
- A/R – how much money you think clients are going to pay you

And add a little more

- What bills you are going to need to pay in the coming weeks

And you start to combine it.

---

[9] Sam is his real name, and that is his real collection rate. He doesn't mind a little positive, public, written praise! And neither would you if your collection rate was this high.

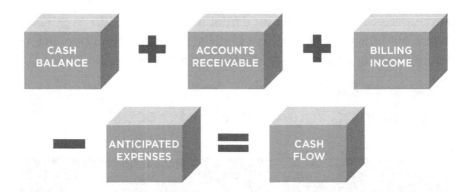

With this information, we can predict how much income we will earn, subtract the bills we need to pay, and then see how much cash we think will be leftover. We do this on a week-by-week basis because revenue and bills are not evenly spaced throughout the month. As everybody knows, the first and third weeks are usually the most expensive because of payroll and rent. The third and fourth weeks usually have the most income (unless, of course, you have a great Fee Agreement in place—then it is the second week). Because of the mismatch, we need to monitor cash levels week by week throughout the month.

Let's go back to Robert. It was his firm that wasn't using any accounting software. After we helped them hire a bookkeeper and she put all the info into an accounting system, Robert was amazed at how great he felt knowing exactly what was in the bank. When we told him we were going to predict weekly balances for the next six to eight weeks, well, he got pretty excited. Once we had everything in place and working, he confided in me that the sense of security was amazing.

It's not always about the sense of security. Sometimes it is about avoiding calamities. Erin,[10] a DUI attorney in Portland, is a great example of this. She had her Cash Flow Forecast up and running when, all of a sudden, it said she was going to run out of money in

---

[10]   Erin is yet another cousin, though this one does happen to be a successful criminal defense attorney in Dallas. I was amazed at the eulogy she gave at her grandmother's funeral (without notes) and said something to my brother. He looked at me and pointed out she was a prosecutor (at the time), and this is what she did all day long. Impressive was the appropriate word.

seven weeks. Let's just pause for a minute. She had SEVEN WEEKS to figure out how to solve her cash crunch. It wasn't seven hours before payroll was due or even seven days, but SEVEN WEEKS.

Maintaining Your Cash Flow Forecast

You are attorneys. Most of you did not spend a lot of time in accounting or business courses, and that's okay. Generally, we advise delegating day-to-day bookkeeping responsibilities to a professional bookkeeper. But when it comes to the CFF, we have different feelings.

If your firm collects below $500,000, you need to be the one to maintain it. Cash is generally tighter, and you need to be close to the numbers. In addition, you are the only one who can make decisions about what gets paid and/or moved if facing a cash crunch. The final reason is cost; it is more cost-effective for you to take 15–30 minutes a week to make adjustments than to give it to a bookkeeper. You would end up spending the same amount of time, plus paying them for their work.

If your practice collects somewhere between $500,000 and $750,000, you can start to delegate maintenance responsibility to your bookkeeper or office manager. Notice that I said delegate. There is a difference between delegation and abdication. When you delegate something, you still need to check in on what is happening, double-check the work product, and ensure everything is going smoothly.

Abdication means you turn it over and simply blame the person when it's wrong. Many attorneys are so happy to have somebody to delegate to that they simply dump tasks in their laps and never follow up. They are annoyed later when the person fails. Unfortunately, it isn't the employee who failed, but the firm owner who abdicated responsibility instead of delegating the task.

After a little hyperventilating and stressing about the red that had shown up on her CFF, we got to work with Erin to solve the problem. The first thing we did was try to move a couple of bills around. The landlord was pretty understanding if rent was delayed for a week, and there were a few others that could be delayed. Unfortunately, it turns out that this cash crunch was more involved than simply moving some bills. We either needed to fire somebody (which we didn't want to do since she needed all of her employees), or we needed more revenue.

We talked about some options, and after we hung up, it was Erin's assignment to think about her current clients and what she could quickly sell to them. We thought she was going to do something typical for a DUI defense attorney and contact past clients who were eligible for an expungement or even start selling it as part of a package to new clients.

Erin was more creative. While she did have her staff mine the files for revenue, she thought about all her clients and why they ended up in her office. For the vast majority, their DUI was a wake-up call that often made them more open to getting help and discovering the true reason for their alcohol abuse. Erin saw an opportunity and was happy to report back on our next call two weeks later that she had solved the cash crunch.

What did she do in two weeks that eliminated such a large shortfall? She designed and sold the "Blue Binder Project." In this program, clients work with a curriculum she designed in conjunction with a therapist to help them deal with the underlying reasons they drink. Once the program is completed, they take their Certificate of Completion to their sentencing, and the judges take that into account. It has been a very popular program for Erin, solved the cash crunch, and continues to contribute to her profitability.

However, it is more important to recognize the number of people the Blue Binder Project has impacted—the many clients who changed their lives and no longer drink. It also impacted their families since the clients received a different sentence than they would have without this program. Erin *literally changed the way people are sentenced for a DUI in Portland.* Why? Because she had a cash crunch and had seven weeks to find a solution.

For detailed information on how to create
a Cash Flow Forecast, see the **How To** section
at the end of the book.

Important Points

- Your cash balance is found in your accounting software, not in an app on your phone.

- A/R is like rotting fruit—the older it is, the less useful it becomes.

- A/R is an uncollateralized loan you are making out of your family's bank account at ZERO percent interest. Stop doing this before you have to explain it to your spouse.

- A/R is created the first time you meet a client. Set expectations by using a Fee Agreement that has a/an:
    - Initial retainer (equal to the first three months of billing)
    - Evergreen retainer (equal to an average of three months billing)
    - Stop-Work policy
    - Ability to withdraw
    - Method to take payment timing out of the clients' hands
    - Credit card authorization form

- Collection rate goals should be 90 percent (but it's higher for our clients).

- Cash Flow Forecast should look 6 to 8 weeks ahead.

- Until your firm grosses between $500,000 and $750,000, you should be the one doing the CFF updates.

Key Number

For most firms, this is the Cash Flow Forecast. It is a forward-looking number that incorporates all other aspects of cash.

Keeping Score

How often do you look at it?

Look at your CFF every week.

What does it tell you?

The CFF tells you if you are going to be short on cash. Make sure you continually look ahead to identify any weeks where you might have a cash crunch.

Give Yourself a Score

- If you don't have a Cash Flow Forecast, give yourself a 0.

- You may give yourself a 1 if you know the approximate amount it costs to run your firm for a month—your "nut."

- If you know what it costs to run your firm in a particular week (for instance, you know that it costs $17,000 the first week of the month, $4,000 in the second week, etc.), then give yourself a 2.

- Firms who start every week knowing how much cash they have, what they expect to get in, what they need to pay, and how much they are going to have leftover at the end of the week have earned a 3.

- You get to give yourself a 4 if you have a CFF that looks out multiple weeks but may have one of these issues:

  - Only looks out a couple of weeks, OR

  - Is consistently off by a significant amount.

- If you have a CFF that looks out six to eight weeks and is accurate (within a few hundred dollars each week), you earned yourself a 5.

On a scale of 0-5, my score is: _____

Why did you give yourself that score?

_____

_____

_____

_____

Results

When a new client comes to CathCap, we always start by looking at cash. What changes need to be made? What can be put in place? How will that ease the client's concerns? In Patricia's case, things changed dramatically. Instead of obsessively checking the app on her phone for her balance and trying to remember every check that had been written, she knows where she stands. After revamping her Fee Agreement (and enforcing it), more money is flowing into her firm without doing any additional work.

This started relieving money pressure she felt at home. Now when she goes home, she can spend time with her spouse and children enjoying the evening instead of trying to figure out how the bills are going to get paid. And most importantly, Patricia knows that this feeling is going to last. She has a Cash Flow Forecast that tells her, in advance, if there are any times when money might get tight again. And in these cases, Patricia knows she has weeks to be able to problem-solve and find the resolution that is right for her.

The CFF is my favorite report for all of these reasons. It is also the one that I personally consult most often. I travel—a lot. While my domestic trips are usually short and only last a few days, my international travel is a different matter. I am usually out of the country for two to three weeks at a time, a couple of times a year. Being able to check my CFF before I leave gives me peace of mind that my business will be fine while I'm gone. Pulling it up on my phone and giving it a quick three-minute check while on vacation lets me know that I can enjoy the rest of my time. No major changes have come up that need to be addressed before I return home.

If you are on vacation at a five-star resort on a remote island with only one update a week—this should be the first Key Number that you check.

CHAPTER 3

IDEAL RATIOS

Once we get cash flow stabilized, we start looking for ways to make the firm more profitable. In Patricia's case, this meant looking at how she was spending her money. While we don't really care what Patricia or any of our clients spend their money on, we do want to make sure that it is a choice that generates a good return for the firm. Ultimately, what Patricia, you, me, and the person sitting on the island want to know is, "What can I spend personally."

The question we are asked most often is, "How much should I be spending on my people (or rent, or marketing, or … you can insert 1,000 other items here). While the first thought that just popped into your mind is probably, "She's going to say, it depends," I'm not.[11] We can answer that question for any business. But what people are really asking is, "How much should I be spending on all this other stuff, because I don't feel like I'm making anything." That question is incredibly important to us. What you are making is what we call Owner Compensation, and it is the Key Number in this chapter.

Nobody reading this book opened a law firm as a hobby. None of you started your business planning to lose money as a tax write-off against your spouse's income. No one started their firm looking for a pro bono job.

You took all the risk to open your firm, and you should be rewarded for that. Our quick and easy answer is, "One-third of gross revenue

---

[11] Remember, I'm not a lawyer.

goes to your people, one-third goes to overhead, and one-third goes to you as profit." That's a pretty easy rule of thumb. We call it the **Rule of Thirds**.[12] Our clients like to get a little more granular than that, so we developed more detailed ratios to help evaluate the health of the firm and determine whether or not the owner is being fairly compensated for their time and risk.

RULE OF THIRDS

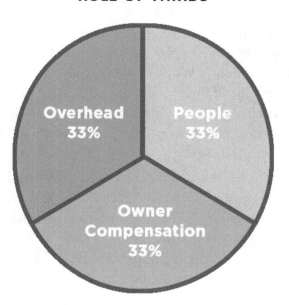

Are the ratios written in stone? The one-third, one-third, one-third pretty much is. Are the more granular ratios fixed? No, they are parameters to keep firms profitable and owners well compensated. They are, however, designed to make you *think* and to serve as *limits* when you make decisions about how to spend money.

---

[12] There are Rules of Thirds all over the place. Most apply to architecture and design. The eye finds spaces divided into thirds or items grouped in odd numbers to be visually pleasing. I find thirds pleasing in finances too.

Ideal Ratios

No matter the size of a firm, a practice needs to balance the same elements—payroll, marketing, operating expenses, etc. As a firm grows, it changes, and how these elements are managed and distributed also changes. As the firm's owner, you need to keep this in mind and be prepared to adapt as your firm evolves.

One of the biggest changes involves your position in the firm. Your job shifts from that of a technician to the role of CEO. As you grow and change, so does your compensation. Less comes from salary because you are doing less billing, and more comes from draws or distributions because you are spending your time and skillset running the firm.

The other thing that changes is the percentage of revenue that your firm spends on marketing. When you are just starting, the majority of your clients come from referrals—professional, former clients, and personal. There is very little expense associated with these beyond the occasional cup of coffee or lunch. In fact, this holds until you near $1 million in revenue. After you pass the $750,000 tipping point, one person can no longer drive that many clients to the firm by themselves. You start expanding marketing activities to include things like print, radio, billboards, pay per click, social media, etc. This creates a big increase in spending. As a firm continues to grow, it builds a reputation, and while your marketing expenses do not go down, they become a smaller percentage of your revenue. Bearing in mind those shifts, let's take a look at our ideal ratios.

People

When most firms start, they usually consist of the founder and possibly a paralegal/assistant. This means that the attorney does virtually everything. He answers the phone (receptionist), types letters to the Court (paralegal), orders legal pads (office manager), does the billing (billing clerk), records deposits (bookkeeper), goes out and prospects for new clients (marketing), conducts sales calls (sales), teaches and trains any staff (senior attorney), and drafts legal documents (attorney). Whew, that is a lot of hats to wear. When you wear a lot of hats, you get paid for them.

In the beginning, the majority of the 33 percent of revenue that goes to payroll is actually going to you, the firm owner. As the firm grows, and you hire people and shed hats, your percentage of that 33 percent shrinks. But that is okay since your paycheck is not diminishing, and you are being paid from other sources (draws or distributions).

We are passionate that only one-third of revenue goes to paying people. Most firms that come to us are closer to 50 percent—and some are even higher. This is the single biggest place where law firms make poor spending decisions. While we want to pay people fairly and want them to feel valued by the firm, we also need to make sure we are getting a good return on our investment.

It is easy to find the return on investment for a billable person. Are they generating (and are you collecting) three to five times what it costs you to employ them? The cost of employment includes taxes and benefits—usually between 12 and 20 percent of their salary. Why multiples of three to five times?

There are three kinds of attorneys—Finders, Minders, and Grinders. Finders are usually partners or more experienced attorneys who go out to find clients and drag them back to the firm. They hand them over to the Minders who take care of them from there. The Minders make sure the client is happy, distribute work to make sure the billable team has enough to do, and supervise, teach, and train younger attorneys. Many firms call these Managing or Senior Attorneys. Some firms call them Non-Equity Partners.

Then there are the Grinders. These are usually the youngest attorneys at a firm, and their job is to grind out hours. If we could get away with it, we would all love to chain them to a desk in an office with no windows and only let them go to the bathroom once a day (maybe).

Grinders are the workhorses of the firm. They are also (usually) the most inexperienced. They need supervision from the Minders, and their hours get written down while they are learning. It might take them longer to get something drafted, but the client is protected by their lower billing rate. The firm also needs to be compensated for the education they are providing. And we do this through the multiple.

Younger attorneys should have a 5X multiple. While still new, they offer little value to the firm beyond their ability to bill. As lawyers grow their skillset, they start to help the firm in other ways. Teaching and training, supervising, and developing new clients are great ways to contribute to the ultimate success of the firm. As an attorney begins to contribute to the firm in ways other than billing, their multiple will fall, but their value rises.

Interestingly, paralegals are the inverse of attorneys. When they start, they don't know as much and are more likely to be tasked with things like filing or picking up the mail. As their skillset grows, they spend more time on billable projects. When creating a compensation package for a paralegal, keep this in mind.

So why not just pay everybody at a 3X multiple of their cost and be done? Why even worry about getting a 5X return since we are going to have one-third of revenue go to people? The answer is that not everybody is billable. The receptionist, bookkeeper, office manager—none of these people can bill enough to pay for themselves. Support staff supports your firm so billers can bill more. Billers need to bill enough over 33 percent to pay for the non-billable staff that is supporting them.

Overhead

Overhead is everything you spend that isn't payroll. Much of this comes from fixed costs, such as rent, phone, and insurance. There are also variable costs, like office supplies and marketing. And of course, there are always a couple of questionable business expenses, such as a car payment/lease, internet for your house, and meals with your family where you discuss the firm. We get it—everybody does it. As long as your CPA is good, we're good.

In general, unless somebody has really expensive space, most firms that come to us are within the 33 percent overhead limits—even with the questionable expenses. That doesn't mean you shouldn't review them on a regular basis. We find that recurring charges tend to creep up. For example, you sign up for a free 30-day trial and forget to cancel. You used a CRM (customer relationship management) software but found something new you liked and didn't cancel the first one because you wanted to try the new one for a couple of months to make sure it was the right decision before canceling the old one ... but then you forgot. These things happen. But they also add up. A $20 charge here and $30 expenditure there, and all of a sudden, it's $1,000 a month—$12,000 a year. Can you find something better to do with $12K a year? Go through the firm's expenditures every few months and just check to see what is there. Most of the waste happens in subscriptions that people have simply forgotten to cancel.

Marketing

Marketing is a subset of overhead in the one-third, one-third, one-third discussion. In a couple of pages, I will show you what we believe to be appropriate amounts to spend on marketing. Before that, I want to explain a few things about the way we approach marketing.

First, the best source of business will always be through referrals. Referrals should be your main marketing plan until you start to approach $750,000. Professional referral sources deliver ideal clients to your doorstep, primed and ready to hire you. Cultivating these relationships is invaluable as you can teach a referral source exactly who your ideal client is. The referral source screens them and then, because they are a trusted resource for the potential client, endorses you! Talk about an easy way to get clients. My father, a corporate litigator, is great at doing this. Over the years, he has cultivated relationships with other lawyers (he seems to know all the divorce attorneys), bankers (they always know when a client is in trouble), and CPAs (who see firsthand when a client is doing something dangerous). These contacts send him a million dollars a year of business, with nothing but check-in phone calls and the occasional lunch.

Client referrals are also a great source. These are people who have firsthand knowledge of how your firm operates. If you aren't getting referrals from past clients, you need to look at the client experience and make some changes. Referrals from friends and family are nice but are not a reliable and constant stream of potential new clients like professional and former client referrals are.

When you do start spending money on marketing, you need a plan. And the plan is not, "I'm going to spend $10,000 on TV ads, and I'll be golden." The plan goes something like this:

I'm going to spend $10,000 a month on TV ads. The station says my ads need to be viewed a certain number of times before people take action, and we hit that saturation point in three months. In month two, I should see some revenue—enough to cover the cost of that month. By month three, I should be seeing a 3X return ($30,000 in revenue). By month four, it will be 6X, and at month six, we should be getting 10X return, or $100,000 of new cases each month. At each stage, you compare projected results with actual results and make decisions about the next step.

I use this example because it is real. Our client Walter[13] wanted to do TV ads for $10K a month, and he didn't have a plan beyond the "I'll get a lot of new clients." Walter did research that indicated results should be steady by the end of the third month. But at the end of month three, he had less than $500 in revenue. Walter spent $30,000 and got a return of less than $500—all of it from paid consultations

---

[13]   Walter is my nephew and Godson. I'm pretty sure he is not practicing law since he is just now turning 3.

with people who did not hire him. We told him to stop, but the TV station must have had great salespeople because they convinced him to go on for two more months. At that point, we think he had revenue of about $2,000. It's important to have a plan with specific milestones, results, and timelines. And then execute the plan!

That is in direct contrast to Alice,[14] who decided she wanted an additional one million in revenue. She knows that each time she cultivates a new professional referral source, they send about $40,000 a year in referrals. That means that she needs to meet and develop a relationship with two new people a month. She has a plan, backed up with data, and is working it! And her business is exploding because of it.

Owner Compensation

As I said at the beginning of the chapter, Owner Compensation is the Key Number. Firm owners care about how much they are being compensated. I specifically use the word compensation here because not all compensation comes in a paycheck. As the owner of the firm, you get paid a number of ways:

- Payroll – compensation for the work you do in the firm.
- Distributions – compensation for the risk you take as the owner.
- Perks – you all bury a few personal expenses in the business' expenses. Don't bother to deny it. And it is fine with us as long as it is okay with your tax accountant. It is still a form of compensation.

Each of these compensates you for a different part of the job that you do. What's important is that you are gaining value from your firm.

---

[14] Yet another cousin. She goes to estate sales and sells the things she finds on Instagram. We think she is cleaning up!

When we talk about the Rule of Thirds, with one-third going to profit, this is the number that really excites our clients because this is what they get to "take home."[15] In reality, total compensation for an owner is often more than 33 percent. They get paid a salary for billable work, which is included in the payroll section. There are expenses that are paid (tax-free) in the overhead section. And then there is profit. In smaller firms, Total Owner Compensation should be around 70 percent, eventually falling to 35 percent once a firm hits five million dollars.

In our granular look at the optimal way for firms to spend money, Owner Compensation shows up on multiple lines:

- Payroll – the portion of your salary that you are being paid for doing billable work.

- Owner's Pay – salary that is for managing the firm, doing marketing activities, and all the expenses being run through the firm.

- Tax – so many firms forget about taxes, and the owners take all the profit, live on it throughout the year, then have a really unpleasant conversation with their accountant every April.

- Debt – many people will question why I consider money used to pay down debt an owner benefit. I do it because you probably signed a personal guarantee to get the loan, so paying it off benefits you.

- Profit – this technically goes to the owner, at least according to the IRS, who taxes you based on this number. However, we do like to leave some of the profit sitting in the firm's account as a war chest and insurance.

---

[15] They don't actually get to take home all of it. The government requires you to pay a portion of it in taxes. Sorry …

Owner Compensation Make-Up
as a percent of revenue

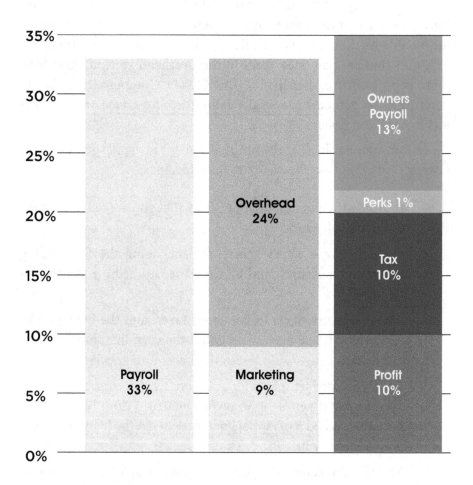

Most attorneys don't know the full value the firm is giving them since so many of the numbers are "buried" and don't show up in their bank account. However, we believe it is important to understand all the benefits your firm gives you.

> It is important to understand all the benefits your firm gives you.

I mentioned earlier that our clients like to get more granular when we discuss how to spend money, so we developed what we call the Profit Finder. I read a book 4–5 years ago

> Profit isn't always about money.

called *Profit First,* and the whole way through, I kept thinking to myself, "Mike,[16] you are speaking my language!". That's part of the reason I was so excited when Mike gave me a quote for the book. Mike M. also believes in the rule of thirds, but he made it more granular. As a numbers/rules girl, I loved the idea of giving more structure to the rule of thirds, so I took a deep dive into what he was saying. Ultimately, I realized his grid needed to change a little to fit the firms with whom we work. Over the past few years, my team and I have worked to refine what Mike started, and our clients (and my team) really love the results.

This grid, divided into revenue bands, looks at where you are spending money and makes recommendations about increasing or lowering the amounts. It starts with the Rule of Thirds but is significantly more sophisticated. Keep reading and you will see this grid. If, after reading this next section, you want to see how your firm is doing, go to CathCap.com/PanictoProfitResources, and you can download your own Profit Finder to tell you where you are over/under spending and get some best practices to help you improve.

$0 – $250K in Revenue

This is a firm that falls into the category of solopreneur. It is generally one attorney and maybe a part-time legal assistant who answers phones, files, does clerical work, and possibly does some light drafting. The majority of the 40 percent payroll is the owner's salary.[17] Marketing

---

16 Mike is Mike Michalowicz, or Mike M, as our team refers to him.

17 If you took an S-Corp election, which most firms in the table generally have, the IRS requires you to take a "reasonable" salary. Unfortunately, the IRS has not given guidance on the definition of "reasonable," so you need to work with your tax accountant to determine what reasonable means for you. A safe bet is to determine how much you would have the pay somebody to do all the billing you are doing.

What is Profit?

There are two kinds of profit. One is the more traditional cash profit. This is what your CPA, the IRS, the bank, and your creditors want to see.

But profit isn't always about money. There is a second kind of profit that is equally important, and only you can define it for yourself. One of the first things we do with new clients is to help them find their definition of profit. We have gotten some great responses. We had a client in Austin who wanted to go to her daughter's swim lessons every Wednesday morning. This meant we needed to build a firm with enough attorneys that somebody else could go to court for her. For this attorney, profit was time with her family.

Another client defined profit completely differently. She wanted to make an impact and change the way stay-at-home wives of high net worth men were compensated, treated, and felt while going through a divorce. To do this, she needed to take national cases. She required a completely different type of firm—one where she was not involved in any part of the sales process since she was planning to be on the road so much. For her, profit was the freedom to pursue her passion.

And ladies aren't the only ones who have a nontraditional definition of profit. A tax attorney in California made attorneys in other states move an offsite meeting so he could attend his daughter's fifth-grade graduation (profit = family). And then, of course, there's the client who wanted to drive past his ex-wife's house in his blue convertible Rolls Royce. To each his own—we don't judge. We just help our clients achieve their definition of profit.

expenses are low because the attorney is out talking to people to hustle new clients, not paying for advertising. Paid marketing expenses might include a listing with an online referral source.

Rent and software are the biggest expenses in the firm, but the total overhead is not too high. The owner not only gets his or her salary, but also gets about 12 percent profit, plus 10 percent of revenue goes in their pocket to pay taxes. Five percent of revenue should stay in the firm's account to form a cash cushion and to fund the next stage of growth. Overall, the owner should be receiving (and paying tax on) approximately 70 percent of revenue.

Some people get confused when they first read this. Their question is, "What happened to the rule of thirds?" Here is how it breaks down:

- 40% is going to payroll – you as the solopreneur are being paid as an employee (this also potentially includes a part-time assistant).
- 28% is going to operating expenses, plus 5% to marketing, gets you to 33% overhead.
- 12% of owner's pay, 10% tax, and 5% profit adds up to 27%. While not exactly one-third, one-third, one-third, it is pretty close.

$250 – $500K in Revenue

We have employees! The attorney has been joined by a full-time administrative person who can also do billable tasks. He/she might be starting to look for a new attorney since a single attorney who bills hourly usually tops out at approximately $350K a year. The firm has started to add some marketing costs such as SEO and small, community-based sponsorships that further cement referral relationships. Operating expenses stay approximately the same in terms of percentages, as does owner's pay.

Taxes stay at a steady rate of 10 percent. One of the interesting things we see is that as a firm becomes more profitable, owners are slow to pay their quarterly taxes. In the previous stage of growth, there is not a lot of profit in terms of dollars, and a lot of families have enough deductions that the tax bill is low. Owners carry this experience forward, without realizing that their tax status has radically changed. This causes a big bill in April that is often hard to pay, which means they get behind and have a hard time getting caught up again. Please always set aside 10 percent of revenue to pay taxes—otherwise, you may be digging a hole that will be hard to get out of.

The profit we leave in the firm grows slightly since the next stage of growth is generally the hardest and most expensive.

$500K – $1Million

It is said that it is harder to go from $500,000 to $1 million than it is to go from $1 million to $5 million, and I believe that. During this period of financial growth, a firm needs to drastically change the way it operates. There are a lot more people on staff, though the percent of revenue drops because the ratio of billable to non-billable people rises. One receptionist can support two or twenty-two attorneys. Marketing costs also increase. There are only so many clients an attorney can bring into the firm by him/herself. As they approach the $1MM mark, they rely on more digital and/ or traditional marketing methods. They also might hire a sales and marketing person and are (hopefully) leveraging their associates to originate clients and paying them a bonus for that.

Taxes

I love to see my clients pay more in taxes. Don't get me wrong, I don't want to pay one more penny than is necessary, but when you are obligated to pay more in taxes, it means we are doing our job. The firm is becoming more profitable, and clients are feeling more financially secure. That's a big win for everybody.

Owners usually freak out when they see their total compensation drops to "only" 50 percent. But wouldn't you much rather have 50 percent of $800,000 ($400,000) than 70 percent of $200,000 ($140,000)? The biggest problem we see with owners at this stage is that they start to "starve" their firms. The firms are finally profitable and are throwing off a decent amount of cash. The attorneys feel more comfortable and start spending more money at home. A lot more money. This is especially true as they start to approach the $1 million mark—there are new cars, new houses, fancy trips, and a general increase in spending. They feel "successful" and feel that they are entitled to all the trappings a "successful" person has.

The problem is that there are also a lot of expenses associated with this growth. New employees must be paid before we have time to bill and collect their time. And more cases means more employees, which means more space. Moving is an expensive proposition, and there are a lot of costs that don't show up on your P&L. Firms need a cash reserve to get through these periods. Generally, you need to make a large cash outlay before a big revenue increase. And if the owner has increased their personal lifestyle, the firm may not have the money to make those large investments. At this point, the firm is starving for the cash that the owner is using to fund his/her personal life.

This is also a stage where we will often see a lot of attorneys get behind on their taxes—especially when firms grow quickly. Attorneys don't stay in close contact with their tax accountants and continue to pay taxes based on the previous year—even when their revenue has doubled.

$1 Million Plus

Economies of scale take over as you hit the one million mark. The firm continues to add more billable people than non-billable, so payroll percentages drop. There are online efficiencies, and the firm has established a reputation for itself, so while marketing spending grows, it grows at a smaller rate than revenue. Operating expenses initially

Profit Finder Percentages by Revenue Level

Total Owner Comp includes estimate for portion of payroll attributed to atty work performed by owner

Real Revenue Range	$ - to $ 250,000	$250,000 to $500,000	$500,000 to $1,000,000	$1,000,000 to $5,000,000	$5,000,000 to $10,000,000
Payroll	40%	40%	35%	33%	33%
Marketing	5%	7%	10%	9%	8%
Operating Expenses	28%	26%	25%	25%	25%
Owner's Pay	12%	10%	10%	10%	9%
Tax	10%	10%	10%	10%	10%
Debt Reduction					
Profit	5%	7%	10%	13%	15%
Total Owner Comp	70%	60%	50%	35%	35%

rise, only to start to fall again. What is interesting is that tax bills rise. As firms grow, the owners are propelled into higher and higher tax brackets. We work with clients' tax attorneys each quarter to see if we need to adjust the amount we are putting aside for taxes. We can't stand April surprises.

Important Points

- Remember the Rule of Thirds:
    - One-third goes to payroll.
    - One-third goes to overhead.
    - One-third goes to profit.
- As the Owner, you get paid in a number of different ways to reflect the different roles you play in the firm.
- How you get paid changes with the growth of your firm and the change in your activities.
- Billable people should bill *and collect* between 3 to 5 times the cost of employing them to support the non-billable people in your firm.
- Before $750,000 in revenue, most clients come from referrals.
- Have a plan for marketing spending. What should this expenditure generate in a specific amount of time? If it doesn't hit the targets, stop the activity.
- Don't starve your firm as it grows—be sure to leave some of the profit in the firm to fund future growth initiatives.

Key Number

The number we all care about is Owner Compensation. Is the firm paying you an appropriate amount of money for the effort you are putting in and the risk you have taken on?

Keeping Score

How often do you look at it?

Look at all the Key Ratios once a month when you review your P&L.

What does it tell you?

The Key Ratios — or even better, the Profit Finder—address where you may be spending in a way that is not efficient. This affects what you have to spend at home.

Give Yourself A Score

- If you have never thought about the percentages you are spending in different parts of your firm, give yourself a 0.

- You may give yourself a 1 if you have ever tried to figure out what appropriate ratios are.

- If you consistently set aside money for taxes every time you take a draw, then give yourself a 2.

- Firms who look at their ratios and try to manage them in some way plus have a marketing plan have earned a 3.

- You get to give yourself a 4 if you have goals for the ratios in your firm, compare that to actuals every month and use your marketing plan to make decisions about continuing marketing activities.

- If you religiously look at your ratios every month and have determined that what you are taking from the firm in salary, draws, and perks is enough to for you at home and to pay taxes, while still leaving half the profit in the firm, you have earned yourself a 5.

On a scale of 0-5, my score is: _____

Why did you give yourself that score?

_____

_____

_____

_____

Results

Clients tend to come to us when they are struggling. Recently, more and more people have unwittingly starved their firm by the time they meet us. Emmy[18] was in this situation until recently. She had a number of the problems mentioned in this chapter, and ultimately, the place she was feeling it was at home. Her personal lifestyle had grown in recent years, and to fund it, she ignored her taxes and racked up credit card debt. This was compounded by the fact that she was spending significantly north of 33 percent on payroll. Her revenue has been over $1MM for a few years and continues to grow steadily. Her bank account was always on empty, so her bookkeeper spent hours each week hoping, praying, and moving money and bills around to make ends meet.

It is rare that owners want to see (or are willing to let) their personal spending diminish after it rises. We needed to pay two years' worth of taxes in one year without Emmy racking up more debt at home and without her feeling deprived at home. Here is what we did:

- Since she was an S-Corp, we started with payroll and had all of her salary go straight to paying taxes. Yes, 100% of her paycheck goes to the government. We did this so she wouldn't be tempted to raid the tax account (usually seen as a cash stash), and we could be confident that we were banking money with the IRS for this year's taxes.

---

[18]   Emmy is an amazing cousin. When she graduated from UVA, she moved to Africa and worked in an orphanage for two years. She continues to teach here in Fort Worth at a small private school that only enrolls students from disadvantaged neighborhoods.

- We talked to her accountant and had him set up a payment plan to settle last year's taxes. We then set up an automatic debit for that amount and put it in her Cash Flow Forecast to ensure it got paid.

- To tackle her payroll problem, we took a slightly different approach. You can't cut people's salaries and expect them to be happy, productive employees. But what we discovered when we did some digging, was not that her team was overpaid, they were just underproducing. Through a series of weekly, one-on-one conversations, their production increased—and so have her collections.

In one year, Emmy paid two years of taxes (this is HUGE), plus, with her collection up, she actually has cash in the bank. Last time we checked, it was almost $90,000. And that was after she ran payroll. She is calmer and more confident. There is a cash cushion in her account, so her bookkeeper is spending half the time she previously was on the books (that means her monthly bookkeeping bill is down). She recently upped the amount of her draw so she can start paying down debt at home, and there aren't going to be any ugly conversations about taxes come April.

While Emmy still has some catching up to do before she can sit on that remote island and make a decision about staying another week, she is definitely on her way. She knows that money is going towards taxes every month, her back taxes are paid, her personal expenses are being met, there is a cash cushion in her bank account, her payroll is inching towards that magical 33 percent, and she did it all because we started looking at her ratios.

CHAPTER 4

PRODUCING LEGAL SERVICES

I had an initial phone call with a new client in Florida years ago who was on a quest to hit the elusive seven-figure barrier—and he was getting close. His biggest problem was that his expenses outstripped (by far) his revenue. Marshall[19] is a bankruptcy attorney who believes in automating and implementing workflows. Since he anticipated hitting seven figures (that's ONE MILLION DOLLARS [20]), he staffed up to be able to handle the additional work.

When we started, we took an inventory of his people and were shocked at the number. Marshall told us they were all insanely busy. So busy, in fact, that he hired a guy who was taking night classes at the local junior college to run around the office all day with a clipboard to make sure all the attorneys were completing the tasks Marshall assigned every morning.[21]

---

[19]   Marshall is my second cousin. He *loves* playing soccer and made varsity as a freshman. He is going to be the team captain for the next three years. Go Marsh!

[20]   I really wanted to put a photo of Dr. Evil from Austin Powers here, but it just wasn't feasible.

[21]   Managing People Tip #1: Let's be real here. There is not an attorney on earth who is going to respond well to some pimply-faced teenager who hasn't even finished college telling him what he (or she) needs to be doing.
Managing People Tip #2: No pimply-faced teenager is going to like being put in the position of telling adults who resent him what they should be doing. And if he does like it, then he is going to be a total A$$ to all the attorneys. Bottom line, this is a recipe for revolt and disaster. Avoid at all costs.

We quickly drafted what we call a billing grid,[22] and gave Marshall a little bad news. He had enough staff to bill *TWO MILLION DOLLARS*. He was totally confused. How were his people so busy but doing so little work? Here's a little secret: When people are getting paid well for a totally cushy job, where they don't have to do much, have plenty of time to arrange their social life, and get to watch *Friends* reruns at the office all day, they aren't going to complain—especially if there are no consequences to this behavior. Within hours, we had decided who was being termed and who got to stay on. Pimply-Faced Teenager was first on our list (no surprise), but the big surprise was that he was the employee Marshall was most afraid of firing. By the way, Marshall turned a profit the very next pay period. This brings me to the topic of goals, capacity, employee productivity or utilization, realization, and the way to monitor all of these in real-time WIP (Work In Progress).

How much work can your firm move through in one week, month, or year? Are your employees productive? And how do you know? Are you invoicing all the work they are doing? Marshall made two critical mistakes. The first was not understanding how much work a person could produce. It took his employees significantly longer to do something than it took him. He rationalized six ways to Sunday (mostly that they were young and inexperienced and would improve quickly) and ignored that little voice in the back of his head that kept saying something is fishy here. His second mistake was not setting goals and holding his people accountable. Marshall needed to know the *capacity* of his firm and how much of that capacity he was *utilizing*.

Billing Goals

I don't care what kind of firm you have; *every billable employee needs a billing goal.*[23] Let's go ahead and address all the objections going through your head before I go any further.

---

[22] If you have questions about creating a billing grid, hold on for a few pages. I'll teach you how to do one.

[23] Billable employees are any employees who do client-facing work. This includes attorneys, paralegals, analysts, etc. It does not include the receptionist, any part of your sales process, or the person that puts all the files back in the cabinet at the end of the day.

Hourly Attorneys

I worked at a big firm where we had to bill 2,000 hours a year just to keep our jobs, and I hated it. I don't want to run a firm where I know the associates are sleeping on my couch every night and cussing out my very existence. You don't have to work your people to the bone. You can have a profitable firm with much lower billing goals that encourage work-life balance.

Contingency Attorneys

We are contingency—what kind of goal can I give since my people don't track their time? Every attorney and paralegal should track their time. It allows you to see which cases are the most profitable (and it's not always the biggest fee cases). Plus, it is extremely helpful from an HR perspective. I'll talk about that more a little later.

Flat Fee Practices

What kind of goal can I give my billable people? The whole reason I went to flat fee billing was so we wouldn't have to track time. ALTERNATIVE: My practice area (criminal, bankruptcy, immigration, etc.) never tracks time. Even if I told my people to do it, they don't know how. I don't even have the software, and everyone would quit. Nobody ever said a billable goal had to be measured in terms of hours.

I understand all of your objections—and I have an answer for each of them. Before we do that, I want to take a look at the billable hour.

The Origin of the Billable Hour

First, I want to establish that the billable hour is a fairly new invention in the legal world and that a single Supreme Court decision made it the dominant form of billing. In 1914, Boston Legal Aid hired a man named Reginald Heber Smith, a Harvard graduate, to bring "scientific management" to the embattled organization.

Within a few years, he had developed both timesheets (in the easily recognizable six-minute increments) and the billable hour as cost-accounting tools. For those of you who skipped the accounting classes, that means he was using them as an internal guide to measure the productivity of his attorneys. It obviously worked, as Boston Legal Aid is still operating, over 100 years later.

Smith did not intend for these to be billing tools. At the time, most attorneys were billing on minimum flat fee schedules set by the courts and the ABA. In 1945, the New York firm of Shearman and Sterling began using timesheets as a way to measure the profitability of those flat fees and to manage their "inventory"—basically the working hours their attorneys had. At some point, attorneys started moving from comparing billable hours to the flat fee charged to simply using the hours to bill. The last of the holdouts fell in 1975 when the Supreme Court handed down a ruling in Goldfarb v. Virginia State Bar, saying that minimum-fee schedules violated federal antitrust laws. At this point, the billable hour was the way forward.

Please note, neither of the organizations credited (accused?) with pioneering the billable hour meant it as a billing tool. It was simply a way to manage the workloads and productivity of employees. And for that, it cannot be surpassed.

Hourly Billing Goals

Most of the firms with whom we work want their employees to live a balanced life. Coaching little Timmy's baseball team and being home for dinner each night is often the trade-off for high six-figure salaries. And many associates are happy to make it. However, what tends to happen is the associate comes on, bills a lot in the beginning because that is what they are used to doing, and then less and less as the months go by. They start to really enjoy this "balanced life," but pretty soon, the owner feels like the balance has tipped to mostly personal. At this point, we often get calls asking how to correct it. The answer is a billing goal.

We start with the premise that an attorney is going to work forty (40) hours a week (see, I told you no 2,000-hour goals). There is no human on earth who can bill 40 out of 40 hours because of what I call Frictional Time Loss. This is the time it takes to go get a cup of coffee, the time to go the restroom, the few minutes it takes after you hang up the phone with a client to figure out where you were on the brief, or wandering around the file room searching for a file. When Frictional Time Loss is removed, we think billing 30 hours a week (about 75 percent of their time) is a reasonable goal.

A goal of 30 hours a week is great for staff attorneys, but senior attorneys and paralegals are different. They don't spend 100 percent of their time on billable activities. Senior or managing attorneys have the responsibility of teaching and training younger attorneys, managing workloads to ensure everybody is busy, and possibly bringing in new clients. These activities take time away from billing and should be considered in their goals. How many hours a week do you anticipate they will be mentoring younger attorneys? Five hours? Then bump their goal down to 25 hours.

Paralegals are similar in that not all of their time is billable, especially when a firm is small and growing. Many paralegals not only do billable work, but also answer phones, do filing, make copies, run downstairs to pick up the mail, order office supplies, and other tasks that are needed to keep the firm running but don't contribute directly to one particular client. Just like with a managing attorney, how many hours per week do you expect them to spend doing these tasks? Once you have set this number, you can arrive at a realistic goal. Keep in mind that they will probably only bill 75% of the time allocated to billing.

Don't forget to reassess your goals on a regular basis. Yearly is the absolute minimum, especially for positions like paralegals. As you hire more employees for more specific positions (you hired a receptionist, and the paralegal is no longer answering the phone), you need to adjust billable hour goals to make sure they match the current iteration of the job.

Contingency and Flat Fee Practices

As Smith found in the 1910s, you need to understand what your people are doing all day to be able to manage workloads. The billable hour is great at that, but many clients tell me it takes too long, or there would be a rebellion if they implemented traditional timekeeping. For these firms, we get creative.

Nobody actually said the *only* thing you can track is hours. We worked with a PI firm in Omaha, where we tracked settlement brochures. Meredith[24] had a thriving seven-figure plus firm that handled a lot of car accidents and minor injury cases, with most of the work being done by paralegals. We knew that when Emmet,[25] the paralegal, sent a settlement brochure out, it had an average life to payout of just under four months. We were pretty happy with that, and Emmet was our most productive paralegal. Other paralegals had much different stats, ranging from 5 to 14.5 months.

The other number we started tracking was the amount of time that passed from signing up the case to when the settlement brochure was sent out. Some of this timing we can't control, as the injured person has to finish their treatment before we know how much we need to ask for in the suit. However, Emmet once again seemed to move his cases through the system faster than anyone else.

Emmet became our standard. We designed an incentive program to motivate paralegals to work their cases. They had a minimum number of settlement brochures that needed to be sent out each month. Once the minimum was met, employees earned flat dollar amount bonuses[26] for every additional settlement brochure.

---

[24] Moving on from family members to college roommates' names.

[25] Emmet is not a cousin either. I have a friend from high school whose sibling is named Emmet, and I just like it.

[26] Notice that the bonus was a flat fee for an activity. It was not tied in any way to the value of the case and, therefore, is not considered by the Nebraska Bar to be fee sharing. As always, check the Bar rules in your state.

Guess what happened? More settlement brochures went out, the time between when the case was signed and the settlement brochure went out was shortened, and the time between the settlement brochure and payout was also shortened. All of this made the firm more profitable. Even better was what happened with Meredith's staff. A couple of slackers quit because they were being held to standards. This allowed us to hire people who were a better fit for the firm. Her employees either stepped up or stepped out. Either way, we had more work moving through the firm and more revenue coming in the door—all without increasing expenses in any meaningful way.

We didn't make them track their hours. We picked a single simple metric and used that to increase performance.

Attorneys are taught to think of every angle to a problem. You turn things over in your minds looking for every hole. Sometimes the next hole you see is that you don't have one metric that will make a difference.

We have a client in the Pacific Northwest named Chris,[27] who is an immigration attorney. He didn't want to track hours, and he didn't have just one metric to track since his case values varied significantly, so we needed a different option. We took each case, looked at approximately how much time it took to complete, looked at the flat fee he charges for each, and assigned a point value. Each attorney (and paralegal) had a point goal—simple, easy, and no tracking hours required.

Whether it is hours, settlement brochures, or points, what you are measuring is the amount of work you can move through your firm. Until you have a handle on that, profitability will be elusive. Give each person a goal of how many XXXs (hours, settlement brochures, or points) they need to achieve each month, then monitor their goals.

---

[27]   Chris is my ultimate entrepreneur cousin. It started in college when he bought the rights to sell a gambling game called Ante-Up in the US. My family still plays it every Christmas Eve. The only downside is that we all look like we are going to the nearest strip club since you play with one-dollar bills. Look into getting one. The little children LOVE it because they usually clean up.

Building a Billing Grid

For hourly firms, the easiest way to track your capacity (billable time) is the same way Reginald Heber Smith did it—the billable hour. You already collected most of the information you need to build your grid. We are just missing a couple of pieces.

Weeks Worked per Year. Each year has 52 weeks, but very few people work all of them. Most firms give two weeks of vacation. That means we are down to 50 weeks. Then there are all the holidays. Most firms celebrate about 10 days a year. These include New Year's Day, Memorial Day, July 4th, Labor Day, Thanksgiving Day, the day after Thanksgiving, Christmas Eve, Christmas Day, and they usually throw one or two Federal holidays in there to round it out.

That means we are down to 48 weeks. And here is where you really start to look at the culture of your firm. Do you want to be very specific about the days/hours people work, or do you want your employees to have a little more flexibility? I often tell clients that $hit happens— usually to the tune of multiple days a year. The employee gets sick; their child is sick; there is a school play; their flight home from vacation gets canceled, etc. There are all kinds of reasons why employees have valid unplanned absences. Let's be realistic and say life ($hit) happens about two weeks a year. At this point, your employees are working 46 weeks a year. And though that seems like very few weeks, it is realistic. And when we are projecting revenue, we want to be realistic.

Billable Rate. The other missing piece of information is an employee's billable rate. There are a lot of places where you can find information to help you determine an appropriate billable rate. Just about every State Bar does a survey every other year or so to determine average billing rates. You can look up average rates by city size, practice area, years in practice, and size of law firm. You can slice and dice this information six ways to Sunday, but at the end of the day, we don't care what other people are charging, we care about billing your employees out at the rate that is right for *your firm.*

When we first say this to clients, they like the idea that we are talking about rates customized for their firm, but they quickly ask, "How can we set that rate?" We are back to the **Rule of Thirds.** One-third of the money collected goes to the people doing the work, one-third goes to overhead (rent, phones, copier, marketing), and one-third goes to profit. To make this work, we again need to have a 3X to 5X multiple of their full-cost salary on all billable employees. This means that you should be *collecting as revenue* three to five times their full-cost salary.

Let's do a quick review. First, full-cost salary is their salary plus any taxes and benefits you pay. What is the *total* cost to employ this person? The second thing is the multiple. *But Brooke, you said one-third goes to the people doing the work. Why would I need a 5X multiple?* Remember, not all employees are billable. Somebody needs to help you pay for the receptionist and office manager.

Determining an employee's multiple. Think back to the last chapter, where I discussed the life cycle of an attorney and a paralegal. Is the attorney at the beginning of this career (Grinder) and needs to be a 5X? Or are they a managing attorney (Minder) who is older and should be closer to 3X?

Now that we know how much we need to collect for each billable attorney, divide that number by the number of hours they are expected to bill (their billing goal times the number of weeks you expect them to bill). Finally, you get your billable rate.

Let's look at an example:

Salary	$65,000
Bonus (approximately)	$ 7,000
Taxes (12.5%-ish)	$ 9,000
Health Insurance	$ 6,000
401K	$ 2,160
Total Cost of Employment	$89,160

Expected Multiple	4.5 (this is a young attorney)
Multiple X Cost of Employment	$401,220
Billing Goal	1380 (30 hours for 46 weeks)
Estimated Billing Rate	$290.74 per hour

Wow, that's pretty high for a second-year attorney. This is the time when you might take a peek at what other firms are using for billing rates. It's fine to be on the high side, but double is probably a problem. What do the estimated billing rates look like for your attorneys? Does it say your second year should be billing at $562? If so, you have a problem with what you are paying your attorney since that is not a realistic number. Go back and renegotiate his/her salary to something more appropriate. Or consider 2,000 hours as their billable goal.

If you are paying your people reasonable salaries, you should have some viable billable rates in front of you. Now squish them around a little, so they are round numbers. We like billing rates that end in a multiple of 25 (25, 50, 75, 100). Adjust them a little more if you think you can get a higher rate than what the math told you. Beware of pushing the number down. It will do nothing but make your firm less profitable.

Now that you have all the information, it is easy to create a billing grid, which tells you the capacity of your firm. Simply open an Excel worksheet and input the information:

Sample Billing Grid

Staff	Position	Rate	Yearly Goal	Total Billed
Attorney 1	Sr Atty	$ 350	800	$ 280,000
Attorney 2	Atty	$ 300	1200	$ 360,000
Attorney 3	Atty	$ 300	800	$ 240,000
Attorney 4	Atty	$ 275	1200	$ 330,000
Paralegal 1	Sr Paralegal	$ 175	1080	$ 189,000
Paralegal 2	Paralegal	$ 150	1080	$ 162,000
Paralegal 3	Sr Paralegal	$ 175	540	$ 94,500
Paralegal 4	Paralegal	$ 150	350	$ 52,500
Receptionist	Legal Asst	$ 65	60	$ 3,900
Yearly Billable			**7,110**	**$ 1,711,900**
Uncollected Rate		4%	284	68,476
Adjusted Income			**6,826**	**$ 1,643,424**

Download a more detailed Billing Grid at
www.CathCap.com/PanictoProfitResources

As you can see, when you multiply the billing rate times the billing goal times the weeks per year, you learn what each employee should bill per year. When you add up each column, you see your capacity or inventory (hours available to sell) and the value of that inventory (total billed). If you are having trouble creating a billing grid (or don't want to spend the time to create one), you can download one at CathCap.com/PanictoProfitResources for free.

Utilization Rate

Your firm's Utilization Rate tells you how much of the capacity of your firm you are using. Firms calculate this in two different ways:

Hours Worked ÷ Billable Hour Goal

Hours Worked ÷ Total hours in a week (or month or year)

Large firms generally use the second. We feel this is a little unfair as we are asking them to bill a certain number of hours, so that is the only number we care about and want to measure. You can make whatever decision is best for your firm.

Clio is a cloud-based practice management software company that goes to great lengths each year to produce a report on the state of the legal industry for small firms.[28] According to the 2019 report, on average, a law firm's billable employees bill 2.5 hours a day.[29] Assuming the billable goal is 6 hours per day (as it is for most of CathCap's clients), that works out to 42% utilization!

Go back to your billing grid and take a look at your total potential billing. Is that realistic? Are you like Marshall, with double the capacity of the work you think you have? Or do you realize that your team is going to have to bill many more hours than you expected to hit your goals, meaning you need to hire—and fast? How much of the capacity are you using?

Monitoring your utilization allows you to balance being profitable while not overworking your people. We generally say that if your firm is growing, you should aim for a 95–100 percent utilization rate (in other words, the number of hours billed divided by capacity).

---

[28]   Clio is a great practice management solution for small firms. It is cloud based, available from anywhere, and has an app!

[29]   Legal Trends Report Powered by Clio 2019, Clio, Accessed October 25, 2019, https://2b9twj15256023uw4w1i3g6q-wpengine.netdna-ssl.com/wp-content/uploads/2019/10/2019-Legal-Trends-Report.pdf.

Once you hit 105 percent, it is time to hire. We don't want your people working too far beyond their goals for too long. They tend to get cranky and bitter—all those things you felt when you had to bill 2,000+ hours a year.

> Monitoring your utilization allows you to balance being profitable while not overworking your people.

There are always exceptions to this. Occasionally, you have an employee who is uber-productive and regularly bills over their goal. If they are happy to do that, incentivize them to continue. By the way, the billing grid at CathCap.com/PanictoProfitResources also computes your utilization.

Work In Progress. Now that you have billable goals for your firm, and you understand the potential of your firm, you need to hold each individual team member accountable for their portion. Goals are worthless if they aren't being tracked. On a very regular basis—we suggest weekly—you need to update everybody on their progress.

Here is where we get to our Key Number—the WIP Report. All practice management systems are designed to track time, and there is a standard report showing how much unbilled time you have per employee. Unbilled time today is next month's income collected. By monitoring how much WIP you have, you are calculating next month's revenue. Nothing is better than the moment in the month when you look at a WIP Report and realize you have more in WIP than your monthly nut, and every hour worked (and therefore dollar billed) from that point on is going straight into *your* pocket.

Run this report and hand it out to each billable employee once a week. If you are using a single metric or the point system, create a report for that (it will probably be in Excel). Are they on track? If not, why not? And how can you help them succeed? If they are on track or over, that should be a small celebration—at the very least, an acknowledgment of a job well done. Because that means you are making more money.

Realization Rate

As all attorneys know, just because an hour has been worked doesn't mean it will be billed. Write-downs, write-offs, no bills, and discounts all mean that the firm does not bill out all hours worked. The hours that make it through the billing process are called the Realization Rate.

Hours Invoiced ÷ Hours Worked = Realization Rate

Clio's Legal Trends Report suggests that only 81 percent of hours worked get billed.[30] This number frustrates me. The analogy I like to use is one where a car dealership gives away one out of five cars. First, I want to be the fifth person who walks onto the lot and gets a free car. But more importantly, what dealership (or law firm) can afford that?

The big question is, "What happens to the hours?" When surveyed, attorneys gave the following reasons:

- Empathy for the client   71%
- Client's ability to pay   59%
- Too much time was tracked   44%
- Concerned the client will object 28%
- Court or Industry guidelines   17%

Small law firm owners are amazingly empathetic. The CathCap team sees it on a regular basis. The problem is, most firms can't afford to give away as many of their services as they do. We ran into this problem with a client in Georgia named Katherine.[31] Katherine runs a

---

[30] Legal Trends Report Powered by Clio 2019, Clio, Accessed October 25, 2019, https://2b9twj15256023uw4w1i3g6q-wpengine.netdna-ssl.com/wp-content/uploads/2019/10/2019-Legal-Trends-Report.pdf.

[31] Katherine was my great grandmother. This is also the name I use when I need an alter ego. I worked for my mother at one point as a personal assistant, and my great uncle thought it was so funny I was using his mother's name, that he called me Katherine until the day he died.

probate litigation firm and is a whiz at marketing. This means that she always has plenty of clients. Unfortunately, their stories touch a place in her heart.

When Katherine's uncle died, he left money to his second wife, but his children challenged the will, and the aunt ended up with nothing. Needless to say, the only people who won in that battle were the attorneys. As a result, Katherine feels for each client who has been taken advantage of in the probate process. Unfortunately, this means she takes cases where the client can't pay (Reason 2 above) or that she wants to help because she feels empathy for their position (Reason 1). The problem for us was figuring out how to avoid cash crunches.

The solution was to create a budget for and make conscious decisions about pro bono work. And we framed it as pro bono. Katherine can have as many as, but not exceeding, five of these cases at any time. The result is twofold. First, profitability has skyrocketed. We aren't constantly juggling bills to keep enough cash in the bank. The second result is the type of cases she takes. Knowing that she can only have five, she is much more selective about the ones she takes. As a result, Katherine selects cases where her involvement has a much larger impact on the families she is helping. This has become part of her firm culture and a reason she is able to keep so many long-term employees. They are "doing good while doing well."

Efficiency

When we put these numbers together, we start to get a better picture of how efficient a firm is with their most valuable asset—billable hours. It also shows us what the effective billable rate is for a firm.[32]

This is how all the numbers play out:[33]

---

[32]   This is what you are actually collecting per billable hour worked.

[33]   Legal Trends Report Powered by Clio 2019, Clio, Accessed October 25, 2019, https://2b9twj15256023uw4w1i3g6q-wpengine.netdna-ssl.com/wp-content/uploads/2019/10/2019-Legal-Trends-Report.pdf.

Ratio	Effective Ratio	Rate	Effective Rate
Utilization	42%	$300.00	$126.00
Realization	81%	$126.00	$102.06
Collection	86%	$102.06	$ 87.77
Total	**29.26%**		**$ 87.77**

These are completely demoralizing numbers, and I want to explain why. For every hour you are supposed to bill, you collect about $87.77. On a billable rate of $300 per hour!

Being efficient with your time and your team's time is the make-or-break number for a law firm. If your team has an efficiency rating of 29% (like the average described above), your firm will be crushed by payroll expenses. That is exactly

> Being efficient with your time and your team's time is the make-or-break number for a law firm.

what Marshall did when he ended up with $2 million of capacity and $750,000 of collections. His rate was 37.5 percent—WHICH IS BETTER THAN THE NATIONAL AVERAGE!

Where should these numbers be? This is what we recommend for our clients:

Ratio	Effective Ratio	Rate	Effective Rate
Utilization	95%	$300.00	$285.00
Realization	90%	$285.00	$256.50
Collection	92%	$256.50	$235.98
Total	**78.66%**		**$235.98**

When we help clients take their Utilization Rate from an average of 40 percent to 95 percent, it has a drastic (and positive) effect on the firm. Holding all other numbers (Realization and Collection Rates) steady, raising the Utilization Rate increases the effective billing rate to $235.98. That's almost 2.5 times what it was before.

Important Points

- Each employee should have a billing goal.

- Billing goals can be hours, a single metric, or even a point system.

- Decide how many weeks per year you want an employee to work.

- Create a Billing Grid to see how much Capacity your firm has.

- Print a WIP report once a week to hold employees accountable and manage your Capacity.

- The Utilization Rate is the percentage of billing goals that are met.

- Monitor billed hours to Capacity to ensure your Utilization Rate is on track.

- Use Capacity and Utilization to determine hiring and firing timing of billable employees.

- Realization Rates represent the percentage of hours worked that are invoiced.

- The most common reason a lawyer writes down work is because they have empathy for the client.

- Create a budget for pro bono work so you can "Do good while doing well."

- Collection rates are the amount collected from what is billed.

- Effective Billable Hourly rate is, on average, the amount collected for every hour that *should have been billed*.

- Of the three numbers, increasing your Utilization Rate has the biggest impact on firm profitability.

Key Number

Most firms use their WIP report as their Key Number. It holds employees accountable plus tells you what next month's revenue will be.

Keeping Score

How often do you look at it?

Look at your WIP report (or your firm's equivalent) once a week. Forever.

What does it tell you?

How much you are going to bill (and therefore be able to collect) at the next billing cycle.

Give Yourself A Score

- If you don't track time or any other metric to be able to hold your team accountable, you get a 0.
- You get a 1 if you track time or another form of production, but your employees don't have goals.
- If you have billing goals but have not looked at them since they were assigned, you get a 2.
- Firms who gave out billing goals but only look at them sporadically, get a 3.
- If all billable employees have a billing goal and they get a WIP report once a week to show their progress and next month's revenue, you get a 4.
- When all employees have a billing goal, are held accountable weekly by reviewing WIP, and you have a billing grid that says you are appropriately staffed for your goals this year, you can give yourself a 5.

On a scale of 0-5, my score is: _____

Why did you give yourself that score?

_____

_____

_____

_____

Results

The purpose of tracking employee profitability is multipronged. The first is from an HR standpoint. You want to make sure that your employees are productive and profitable. If you don't track what they are doing, they will be "busy," but work won't move through your firm. The second reason is related to the first. By creating a Billing Grid, you can see if you are over or understaffed for the goals you set for the year. The last reason is for planning purposes. By looking at your WIP report on a weekly basis, you have an idea of what this month's billing, and therefore next month's revenue, will look like. Confidently knowing next month's revenue is what allows you to make a decision about staying on the island.

How Goals Help HR

Have you ever had an employee who was kind of annoying? They get their work done, but not as quickly as you would like. They show up, mostly on time, but not so late that you can write them up for it. They move slower than molasses in January, even under deadline. They spend a lot of time leaning on people's door frames, chatting. They are there, but their attitude is, at best, blah.

It is hard to fire marginal employees—unless you start looking at their productivity. Marginal employees almost always miss their billing goals. If you have an employee you don't love, give out billing goals, and hold everybody accountable. The marginal employee will be out in just a few pay periods.

CHAPTER 5

BUDGET VS. ACTUAL

I am a numbers geek—I accept that and wear the title proudly. And while I shouldn't have favorites among our "numbers," I do. And this is it. Most accounting software programs call this number Budget vs. Actual, and it is where we get to see if our projections were right.

Every report we have looked at thus far has told us either what happened or what we think is going to happen. We spend a lot of time trying to project the future when we look at our WIP report, project our A/R, and try to figure out how much cash we are going to have at the end of any given week. But none of those projections is any good if we don't take a step back and ask, "Were we right?"

I often get asked, "Does it even matter?" The answer is yes, for a couple of reasons.

1. Don't spend time working on projections if you aren't going to use them.

2. If you don't check the accuracy of your projections, you run the risk of making decisions based on faulty data.

> Don't spend time working on projections if you aren't going to use them.

A few years ago, I was working with a client named John[34] who was a genius at marketing. Don't ask me his secret. I don't know exactly what it was. He spent ZERO money on the internet (though he did have a website). He did not pay to advertise anywhere but in the yellow pages.[35] He didn't even have a newsletter! What he did do was go out and meet people in his community, and client by happy client, he built his reputation. This is usually the best use of time and is the marketing source that is most effective. What made John different was his ability to build those referral relationships quickly.

John was highly organized and very logical. He liked the projection part of being a business owner, so we built a beautiful Profit Plan (budget), and he even had a business plan. With his firm, we knew how fast he was going to grow, when he would need to hire new people, and even when we thought he was going to have to break his lease to find an office with more space. We put everything in place and watched his firm take off.

Most firms, if they have a budget at all, take a "set it and forget it" approach. They do it once a year and never look at it again. If we had taken that approach with John, it would have been a disaster. The first month out, I looked at his Budget vs. Actual report and was a little surprised. We had trounced our projections. Most people think this is great, and it was, but I started to worry a little. The next month, I realized he was where I thought he would be in four months, not just two. He was growing twice as fast as we thought he would. John and I needed to spring into action because we could see that he needed to hire faster than expected, and he needed to start negotiating his way out of that lease. We had to make adjustments.

---

[34] Okay, there are lots of Johns in my family. My father, my brother, an uncle, and a cousin are all attorneys. There are other Johns (five more, to be exact), but they aren't attorneys. You can decide which John you want this to be.

[35] He spent $10,000 a year on that ad, and it worked like a charm. I was shocked at how effective it was. Who knew there were people who didn't immediately recycle those when they landed on the doorstep?

When I teach Continuing Legal Education (CLE) and get to this part of the 6 Key Numbers®, I usually start talking about rockets, JFK, and getting to the moon. I say that a budget is a living, breathing document that needs to be constantly updated. A rocket needs the same kind of recalibration. NASA doesn't simply program a path into a rocket, fire it off, and hope it makes it to the moon. They set a destination, put in coordinates, then check on a regular basis to make sure the rocket is not off course. If it has drifted, been pushed off course, or is otherwise not where they think or want it to be, they make an adjustment. And those adjustments are what allow the rocket to reach its destination.

> A budget is a living, breathing document that needs to be constantly updated

Your Budget vs. Actual is the report that tells you if your rocket is still on course. In John's case, it wasn't—he was significantly ahead of where we thought he would be, so we made adjustments. It also allowed us to look at our assumptions and make changes going forward so that we would become more accurate.

Every projection is based on assumptions, like marketing activities will give you a certain number of clients, or the average value of a case is XXXXX. If we are working with faulty assumptions, we make poor decisions. The more often we review the product of the assumptions, in addition to the assumptions themselves, the more accurate we become.

It All Starts with a Budget

A budget is a planning document that projects the profit and loss numbers for the coming year. It is usually written in the fourth quarter, and few people have fun making one. The majority of these documents simply sit ignored in a drawer.

A good budget takes many of the 6 Key Numbers we have discussed and brings them together in a meaningful way. It allows us to start to look forward and to be more proactive about where and how money is spent. This budget should be used each month to gauge the progress a firm is making and how well it is doing.

Most law firms grow and develop organically. While an attorney might want to have the "biggest" or "best" law firm in town, there is rarely a plan to make that happen. Some attorneys are very talented at networking and getting referrals. Others might realize that the way to attract clients is through online advertising. And other attorneys are great at working the cases or connecting with clients. And while all of these can help a firm grow, they can only take you so far. Having a particular skill is not a plan.

When new clients come to us, we hear a lot of comments about where they want to go, but it is almost always followed by, "But I don't know how to get there." The reason for this is they don't have a plan. You read all over the internet and in business books that you need a business plan, and while I don't think that is a bad idea, they aren't as useful in day-to-day firm operations as a budget.

Many law firms float, meander, and drift towards success or struggle. And owners often can't tell you how they ended up where they are other than vague references like, "It's worked out," or "I'm good at marketing," or my personal favorite, "I'm lucky." Those attorneys aren't lucky. They are doing things that make them successful. But since they don't have a plan, they can't identify what those things are.

Law firms that work with us have a plan. We know where they are today and where they want to be at any given point in the coming year. We know how many matters they want to have open, how many people they want to employ to work those matters, how much marketing they are going to do, and how much space they will need to house it all.

Does this sound like a business plan? Sort of, but it's not. It's simply the story of your firm. And then we put numbers to those plans. That's the point at which it becomes a budget.

Everyone Hates Budgets!

Okay, I'll say it, because I know you're thinking it. Budgets SUCK! People don't like making budgets for a few reasons, but the biggest one is that budgets are perceived as restrictive. I feel the same way. I don't like anybody or anything telling me what I can't do. And if you are reading this book, then you are an entrepreneur. And entrepreneurs are all about the possibility—not the prohibition.

Remember the *Profit First* book I mentioned? The author, Mike Michalowicz, said something that really changed the way I felt about budgets.[36] He turned the basic profit and loss equation around. Instead of Revenue minus Expenses = Profit, he advocates that it should be:

$$\textbf{Revenue}$$
$$-\ \textbf{Profit}$$
$$=\ \textbf{Expenses}$$

This is genius! It was at that moment that I realized using a budget doesn't mean we are simply planning for profit. Instead, we are planning to cover our expenses. Since the point of every business should be to make a profit, we should plan for that success. That was the moment I threw out the word budget and started using Profit Plan instead. A Profit Plan sounds like more fun. It talks about the profit you will make so you can start planning what you can do with it. Expenses? Those become money you *get* to spend to make your profit. This is definitely more fun than sitting around, thinking you aren't allowed to spend money.

> Since the point of every business should be to make a profit, we should plan for that success

---

[36] As mentioned, I LOVE his work, especially *Profit First*. It has changed the way we help our clients become successful. If you haven't read it, I suggest you go out and buy it now.

But why is a Profit Plan even considered a foundation of the 6 Key Numbers? Yogi Berra said it best: "If you don't know where you're going, you'll end up someplace else." And generally, that someplace else does not involve a smooth-running firm with lots of profit. Your Profit Plan is your goal, your roadmap, your plan for the year. It shows you where you want to go but also helps keep you on course.

Why do I care if you have an accurate (or even inaccurate) Profit Plan? Because it gives you a framework. It gives you a yardstick by which to measure things. It helps you make better decisions. Every day lawyers are presented with opportunities, and the biggest challenge is figuring out whether they will move them closer to or further from their goals. Without a Profit Plan, those decisions are made on gut instinct, not facts. And while, as a whole, I am constantly amazed by the accuracy of attorneys' gut instincts, you do tend to second-guess yourself. This keeps you up at night and distracts you during the day. Creating a Profit Plan gives you a roadmap and some peace of mind.

We've already established that a Profit Plan is nothing but the story of what you want to happen in your business over the coming year with some numbers attached. So, the first step is to sit down and think about what you want your business to look like at the end of the year. Think about how each individual month will need to look in order to build up to your December goals. Once you have done that, you can start building your Profit Plan.

For detailed information on how to create
a Profit Plan, see the **How To** section
at the end of the book.

Using the Budget vs. Actual

This is all pretty theoretical, so let's discuss how to read and use your Budget vs. Actual report most effectively. The first thing you need to realize is the report is nothing more than your budget set next to your P&L. Revenue will be at the top with expenses below. The last line shows how much (if any) money you made this month.

In finance, you always run the risk of getting lost in the numbers and ending up with analysis paralysis. To avoid this, we try to stay as "big picture" with the numbers as possible, so our favorite lines on a P&L or Budget vs. Actual report are always the total lines. Once we look at the big picture, we can make a decision to see if we need to dig down deeper.

I always like to jump to the punch line, so the first thing I do when looking at a Budget vs. Actual report is to go to the last line to see if you made money. The second thing is to compare that number to what we *thought* you were going to make. Is that total above or below the projected number? We always want the actual to be higher than the budgeted Net Income number. But if it's not, why we were off is almost as important as the number itself. And we need to go back up the page to figure out the why.

Revenue

Back up towards the top of the page, the Total Revenue amount will be listed. Ask yourself the same question we did about Net Income—"Am I over or under what I projected?" If you are over, *yea!* If you are under, it's not the best news, but in both cases, we need to find out why. At this point, most of our newer clients ask why we need to look deeper into good numbers—and the answer is simple. We want to find the root cause of bad numbers and fix them. Equally important, we want to find what you did right and repeat it. Finding the activities in your firm that drive your revenue so you can repeat them every month is one of the secrets to a successful (and profitable!) law firm.

Let's start with the scenario where we missed our projections. Firms generally miss revenue projections for just a handful of reasons:

- They didn't have enough work to keep everybody busy.
- They had the work, but the associates didn't hit their billing goals.
- They billed the work, but their clients didn't pay them.

All other reasons are usually a variation of one of these.

If you didn't have enough work, you have a marketing problem. What were your assumptions? Did you not book the number of speeches we thought you were going to? Did you get sick and miss six networking events? Did you spend two weeks of the month in court, so all potential new client sales calls had to wait for a few weeks before they could even see somebody to talk about hiring your firm?

All of these are things that can (and will) naturally happen in a law firm, so a well-prepared firm makes plans to deal with the inevitable. If the speeches weren't booked, put a procedure in place where you work more closely with your assistant to monitor the number of bookings. Make sure you are not the only person who can go to networking events—associates and even paralegals can be great at promoting your firm. One tax attorney's firm administrator is one of the best people she has to go out in public and talk up the firm. Networking doesn't have to be done by you.

The second problem on the list—associates not hitting their goals—is a teaching and training problem. If you have the work, yet they aren't hitting their billing goals, this is the time to dig down and find out why. The biggest problem we see is that more experienced attorneys aren't taking the time to teach younger attorneys how to work a file. Often, there is work there that the newer attorney is just not experienced enough to find. Does your firm have status meetings on files to train younger attorneys on how to spot work? Sometimes you simply have employees who aren't going to raise their hands and say, "I don't have enough to do."

Remember Marshall, the immigration attorney from Florida, and all his "busy" employees? Use your WIP report to make sure this doesn't continue to happen. Also, check to make sure there wasn't a technical problem like the power was down for a week, or your server was hacked and held for ransom. Don't laugh. I have seen firsthand both of these things happen at client firms. Insurance is usually your best friend in these scenarios.

The last problem is A/R. Since we have already discussed this at length, I won't go into it again. However, your Budget vs. Actual report will absolutely show you if you aren't collecting what you thought.

These are the things to look for if you missed revenue projections. But what if you blew it out of the water? You do the exact same thing in reverse. Revenue was up? Was it more cases, employees billing over their goals, or higher collections? Be careful here, because being over your goal is not always a good thing.

Yes, I said that. And I'll say it again—it's not always a good thing. Sometimes being over your revenue goal means you are burning out your people. Let's go back to John and his rapid growth. He had so many cases coming in that he was filling up his attorneys and paralegals twice as fast as we thought he would. Since John lives in a TINY town in the Pacific Northwest where it is hard to find attorneys, I am always concerned that we keep the ones he has happy. Billing 50 hours a week is not part of John's firm culture and not the way he wants to treat the team. When he started growing at this pace, he had to really step up his hiring efforts to avoid having an exhausted and burned out staff. Make sure you are looking at your Utilization and not overworking your people.

If we continue down the list above, the inverse of having the work but not hitting billing goals is not having the work but hitting billing goals anyway. This is another teaching and training moment, but one in which you discuss overworking or overbilling a case. Just because clients have money in trust doesn't mean you should be billing on their matter.

Being over your revenue goal is usually positive, and again, an opportunity to optimize your practice. We suggest our clients track revenue by type of case (cases can be divided into 4–6 types). And we often recommend they track it by referral source within those types. When you have this kind of visibility into your revenue, you become very efficient in the use of your resources. Was there a particular type of case where more matters came in than expected? Reflect back on the marketing you did and see what you did differently—then do it again. And again. And again. Having more cases coming in and understanding what you did to make that happen is one of the hardest, and most important, nuts to crack.

The last point I want to address about being over your revenue goal is your collection rate. What percentage of what you billed was received in 30 days, 60 days, and 90 days? If your collection rate goes up, celebrate this fact with everybody in your office. It is a team accomplishment—buy them lunch!

Expenses

Now that you know why you were over or under on revenue, it is time to do the same with expenses. Look at each category, such as Marketing, Office Operations, and Payroll, and see if you were over or under. Ask yourself the same question, "Was it good or bad that I was over/under?" Over in Office Supplies might be great if it means that your Trust and Estate Practice had to purchase a bunch of binders because you had more clients than usual. Or it could mean that your office manager has socked away enough paperclips to last for the next ten years.[37]

Walkthrough each section and make a list of things that need to be changed and the good activities that need to be repeated. Don't take on all the change at once—find one or two things per month that need a new process or policy and fix those. Optimizing your law firm takes time, and employees become overwhelmed when too much changes at once. It can make them rebel—verbally or simply by not doing what they are supposed to be doing. Either way, it can be catastrophic for your firm. In this case, slow and steady wins the race.

---

[37]   Don't laugh. This actually happened to one of our clients. When the office manager left, they checked her closet and could see why their office supply bill had been so high. Not sure they've needed to buy more supplies yet, and I know they haven't bought paperclips. They won't need more of those for at least a decade.

The last thing I like to do is go back and look at your ratios. How far off are you from the rule of thirds? Are Marketing and Overhead in a good place, but Payroll is too high? Are you able to take out not only the recommended amount but also enough to satisfy your needs at home? Do you have a tax savings account? Going back to these numbers month after month helps to keep you on track to a profitable firm.

Important Points

- It's a Profit Plan, not a budget.
- It is the story of what you want your business to accomplish in the coming year.
- A Profit Plan gives you the ability to see how different things (like marketing expenses or hiring an employee) affect both revenue and expenses.
- It only takes four steps to make one, so no need to panic.
- A Profit Plan is a living breathing document and should be updated each month.
- Your Budget vs. Actual report is your Profit and Loss set next to your Profit Plan.
- Go to the bottom of the report first to see if you made or lost money.
- Return to the top to see how you did on revenue vs. what you planned to deposit.
  - Where were you over and under, and why?
  - How did your marketing efforts affect each of those results?
- Keep going down the report and repeat the process with your expenses.
  - Were you over/under for a good reason? If so, what was the activity that created that result? Repeat each month.

- If you were over/under for a bad reason, what needs to change so it doesn't happen again?
- Decide what one or two things need to be changed this month.
- Revisit your Profit Finder to see how far you are from optimal percentages.

Key Number

The important number here is the Budget vs. Actual report. Using the dreams from your Profit Plan is the key to staying on track to reach your goals.

Keeping Score

How often do you look at it?

Once a month.

What does it tell you?

Where you need to make adjustments to reach your goals.

Give Yourself A Score

- If you don't have a Profit Plan (or a budget), or if you have one that was produced by your bookkeeper based on last year's revenue and expenses, you get kudos for recognizing that you need something—but no points.

- Firms who create their own budget based on projections but stick it in a drawer, get a 1.

- To get a 2, you need to have a detailed plan. A real plan. Not an "I'm going to do $1 million this year" plan with no supporting changes in marketing or staffing approach. Instead, it should be based on trends, *and* you give it to your bookkeeper to put in QuickBooks.

- To get a 3, you need to have a plan that includes your dreams, *and* you look at your Budget vs. Actual every month.

- You get to give yourself a 4 if you review the Budget vs. Actual each month and make changes in your firm to improve next month's number.

- If your bookkeeper produces a Budget vs. Actual report every month, you review it once a month, you analyze it to see what changes need to be made in your firm (and implement them), plus you look ahead to make sure the Profit Plan is right for the next few months, you earned yourself a 5.

On a scale of 0-5, my score is: _____

Why did you give yourself that score?

_____

_____

_____

_____

Results

It is frustrating for firm owners to get to the end of the year and realize that they are in about the same place they were at the end of last year. By using a Profit Plan, firms lay out a path to their desired location. The Budget vs. Actual report tells them how far they have strayed from that path, or where on the path they are in relation to where they wanted to be. It's like a GPS for a firm.

John is a great example of this. By using his Budget vs. Actual, he knew he was much further down the path than he expected to be, and he was able to plan for hiring, moving the office, and other expenses. Had we not been using this to gauge his growth, John would have had more work than he could handle with his current staff. And he wouldn't have had the cash reserves to be able to move to a larger space.

More importantly, John represents the guy who can make the decision to stay on the island and vacation for another week. His Profit Plan and a review of his Budget vs. Actual immediately tells him how the firm is doing. If John did not have a Profit Plan, he might have stayed on the island another week, but he might also have been slightly panicked the whole time—worrying that his staff was overwhelmed, and work was falling through the cracks. Instead, he put on more sunscreen and ordered another umbrella drink.

CHAPTER 6

MARKETING AND SALES

Numbers are fascinating. When I was in grad school, I took a class that taught us how to determine the price of a stock. In the investment world, you use this value to then find stocks priced under your estimate, buy them, and wait for the price to go up. As I was working through the project, I noticed that little changes here and there made a huge difference in my stock price.

In frustration, I called a friend who had worked for Goldman Sachs. After Davey[38] quit laughing, he said that is why it is easier to start at the end number and work backward. This approach of starting with the end number makes sense to me, at least in the world of law firms—maybe less so when you are trying to buy stock. At CathCap, we often start with the end number with our clients.

Remember when we were building the Profit Plan? We came up with a revenue number based (most probably) on the number of people working at your firm. The assumption is that you have sufficient work for them to do. Ensuring that you have the work is a marketing and sales problem. Here's how we breakdown and attack marketing outcomes.

It all depends on your marketing and sales KPIs (Key Performance Indicators). The most important of these is your Conversion Rate. This is the number of prospects that become clients. Most attorneys tell me

---

[38] This is his actual name, and he is kind of my hero. He worked like a dog (who doesn't at Goldman?) and retired at 29. He has managed his own money ever since.

they have an 80%+ conversion rate. While that may be true, they are usually only referring to one part of the equation. Your true conversion rate is a series of small yesses—of people moving to the next step.

> Your true conversion rate is a series of small yesses—of people moving to the next step.

Here are the steps we track:

- First Contact to Qualified
- Qualified to Appointment Set
- Appointment Set to Appointment Show
- Appointment Show to Client

Conversion rates don't just tell us how well your sales process is working (though it does). It also tells us what is and isn't working in your marketing. Let's look at each step, so we have a thorough understanding of each one and why it's important.

What Happens When The Phone Rings

Potencial Client   **No Longer A Prospect**

First Contact to Qualified

Every time the phone rings, and it is not an existing client or opposing counsel, it should be tracked. Track all those calls asking for an attorney to defend them in a drug case, help them with an immigration problem, or asking what to do about a letter from the IRS—even if you have a family law firm. Your receptionist needs to track *every single call.* Yes, I know your receptionist is going to roll her eyes, and you are thinking it is a waste of time to track calls that aren't right for your firm. But that is exactly the point. If you are getting calls for cases that your firm doesn't handle, somewhere in your marketing materials, you're either giving the wrong impression or not being specific enough.

Notice that the heading on this section is First Contact to *Qualified.* The qualified is the important part. Out of every 10, 50, or 100 calls, how many are right for your firm? Your receptionist can ask a few innocuous questions and, in return, receive an immense amount of valuable information. These qualifying questions help ensure you and a potential client are a good fit.

How to Prequalify Prospective Clients

Training your receptionist to ask a few simple, non-threatening questions will save you and potential clients time by making sure you are a good fit. Here are some questions the receptionist should get answers to before scheduling a prospective client meeting:

- Is this the type of law your firm practices?
- Is this the type of case that you like?
- Are you conflicted out?
- How did they hear about you?
- Can they afford to pay you, and if not, who is going to foot the bill?

Of course, they should also get contact information so you can keep them in your sales pipeline.

Think of it this way. How many times have you ended up talking to a prospective client only to figure out that you don't practice their kind of law, you are conflicted out, or they can't afford to pay you? That is a waste of everybody's time—yours and the prospective clients. In your case, it probably cost an hour of billing, which can add up over the course of a year. In the client's case, they leave feeling their time was wasted, which does not engender warm fuzzy feelings about your firm. Asking a few qualifying questions *before* making an appointment for a PNC (potential new client) saves everybody time and hassle.

The percentage of people who are right for your firm is the first indication of how well your marketing plan is working. Your marketing activities are what compel people to contact your firm. When you have a large percentage of people contacting your family law firm to defend a DWI, there is a problem with your marketing. Somehow, you are giving off the wrong impression—and let's be clear—marketing is all about leaving an impression. In general, 40 to 45 percent of all people who contact your firm should be qualified. If the PNC answers all the questions appropriately, move on to the next stage.

Qualified to Set

Not everybody who is qualified will set an appointment with you. The big question for you to answer is why. Tracking the number of people who are interested enough to call you, answer a few easy questions, and then still don't make an appointment can tell you a lot about your firm. On average, 75 percent of qualified people should take the next step. If they aren't, look at a few things:

- **How long does it take to get an appointment?** In many cases, a client can't wait a couple of weeks to see you. They have an upcoming court date or, frankly, are just so worried and panicked that they would rather see somebody further down their list rather than wait for you. Make sure you block out time each week for scheduling PNCs.

- **Do you have a paid consultation?** Sometimes clients will balk at paying $300 to interview you to see if they want to hire you. If this is the case, you need to coach your receptionist on how to present it. If you are still getting pushback from prospects, offer to credit the amount to their first bill. We are *big fans* of paid consultations.

- **Are you too far away?** If this is the reason people aren't booking an appointment, you need to go back and look at your marketing because you are attracting clients who aren't even in your area!

Set to Show

Forty-five percent are qualified, 75 percent make an appointment, but how many are showing up? This should be north of 80 percent of people who made an appointment. If it's not, it is usually easy to fix.

- **Have a paid consultation.** I said we were big fans, and this is why. If potential clients pay $300, you can be pretty confident they are going to show up.

- **Make sure you are easy to find.** This might sound weird, but it is amazing how often attorneys don't think of the client's experience when it comes to finding the office. I went to visit a practice in Pennsylvania for a short one-day consulting gig. I found the building easily enough, parked, and walked up to the front door. It was locked. There was no bell or buzzer to let them know I was there.

  So here I am, standing in front of a building in a parking lot with cars, on the edge of a two-lane highway, completely confused (and feeling like an idiot). I checked my calendar, and yes, I was supposed to be there. I checked the address, and yes, I was in the right place. I finally called the office. They told me to walk around the right corner of the building, go down some steps, and enter by the side door. This is not the type of experience that gives a prospective client a lot of confidence and faith in a firm.[39] Are you easy to find? Is there adequate signage? Can clients quickly and easily locate you without being given the opportunity to second guess this decision?

- **Confirm the appointment.** A couple of confirming emails, texts, or a call could have mitigated my experience in Pennsylvania. We encourage clients to give their PNCs as much information as possible to make them feel confident in their decision. One client in Dallas sends an email a day or two before the appointment that has directions to the office, along with photos showing where to park, how to enter the building, and where their office is. I love it!

  A call the day before to confirm will remind the prospect. If they are going to cancel, they usually do it on that call. While it means you lost a PNC, it also means you get that billable hour back since you won't be sitting around wondering if the PNC is late, lost, or simply not coming.

- **Get information in advance.** Confirmation emails are also a great time to collect some information from the client and help them understand what is going to happen during their appointment. We worked with an estate planning attorney in Florida who spent his whole PNC appointment going through an eight-page list of questions—how boring for everybody involved! Instead of building a rapport with the prospect and getting to know them, he was checking off boxes. We helped him design a series of emails to be sent out *before* the appointment to ask those very same questions. By the time the PNC showed up at his office, our client knew everything he needed about the plan and could spend the time getting to know the client.

---

[39] By the way, I got an email recently saying the practice was closing. I wasn't surprised.

Show to Hire

This is the percentage that most attorneys can rattle off at the drop of a hat (though it is usually gut instinct and a little optimistic). Of all the people who walk into your office and have a sales conversation, how many of them actually sign on the dotted line? By this time, they have jumped through quite a few hoops and said yes a number of times. They should be ready to buy. A conservative goal is a 65 percent rate of hire. If your rate is below this, you need to work on your sales call. Here are some ways to improve your pitch:

- **Take a sales course** online or in person.
- **Have a script**—the most amazing sales call I have ever seen was by an estate attorney here in Fort Worth. I saw him at a party about six months later and told him it was a masterful sales call and recited my favorite part. He picked up at the end of my sentence and kept going. While I am sure he doesn't use the same exact words each time, he does have a plan of what he needs to communicate and in what order to achieve the best results. And, yes, we bought.
- **Presell your client.** That attorney with the script is where I learned about gathering information in advance of the sales call. By the time I showed up, I had submitted so much information he knew more about my family's financial position than we did. I had committed to the process numerous times and shared so much personal information that there was very little chance I would walk out without signing the Fee Agreement.
- **Is the best person doing the sales call?** Sometimes it is hard to sell yourself. It is also hard for attorneys *not* to try and prove how smart they are and how much they know during a sales call. These things can be a turn off for PNCs who really just want to be understood and have somebody say they can fix it. Really evaluate each person in your office as a salesperson.

You might discover someone else can convert better than you (though that is rare).

Overall Conversion Rate

When a firm has a sales process that is working well, its conversion rate looks like this:

Conversion Stage	Goal
Call to Qualified	45%
Qualified to Set	75%
Set to Show	80%
Show to Hire	65%
Overall Conversion Rate	18%

Eighteen percent of all people who contact a firm become clients. While that sounds low, it is harder to achieve than you might think, and it is a great place to be. Remember the beginning of the chapter when I talked about reverse engineering numbers? This is where you start.

Let's say you want to have a $1,000,000 firm. I'm choosing this number because it seems to be the first goal that most fast-growing firms have, and only five percent of businesses in the US make it to that revenue number.[40] The second assumption I am making is an average case value of $8,500. This means that, in general, every case that comes through the firm is worth $8,500.

To reach $1MM in sales, we need 118 cases.

---

[40] 2016 US Census. Total businesses in the US = 30,414,806. Businesses with revenue or receipts over $1MM = 1,535844. Total percentage is 5.05%. https://factfinder.census.gov.

To reach 118 cases, we need 182 sales calls.

To have 118 sales calls show up, we need to book 228 appointments.

To book 228 appointments, we need 304 qualified clients.

To get 304 qualified clients, we need 676 people to call the firm.

What all of this tells us is that if the sales machine is running smoothly, we need approximately 56 people to contact the firm about hiring us each month. The larger question becomes, "What are you doing to make the phone ring 56 times?" If all of this seems like hard math, go to CathCap.com/PanictoProfitResources, and you can download a spreadsheet that does all the calculations for you based on your current conversion rate and this idealized version.

Track Your Marketing Activities

I am a big believer in the phrase, "If you can't measure it, you can't improve it."[41] Just like with your conversion rate, if you track your different marketing opportunities, you'll start to see trends that tell you where you should and shouldn't be spending your time and money.

> If you track your different marketing opportunities, you'll start to see trends that tell you where you should and shouldn't be spending your time and money

Let's look at time first. I was working with Gordon[42] to review his marketing plan for the year. He described all kinds of fun things he wanted to do, and I stopped him. What were the activities that would have the most impact on the firm, and more importantly, how much time did he have to devote to these activities?

---

[41] Some attribute this to Lord Kelvin and some to Peter Drucker. You can decide for yourself who said it (best).

[42] This is another entrepreneurial cousin. He started an analytics company that shows live theaters which shows they should produce based on their audience.

Gordon was already complaining that he worked a lot and couldn't give more hours to the firm, so I wanted to be *very strategic* with how he spent his time. We allocated a certain number of hours per week to marketing. Then, we looked at marketing options to determine how much time each of them took and what type of return to expect. This is what we found:

Activity	Hours per Month	Anticipated Revenue	ROI – Return per hour spent
2 New Referral Sources	30 hours	$ 600,000	$1,667
Webinars	5 hours	$ 72,000	$1,200
Quarterly Events	5 hours	$ 48,000	$ 800
Speaking	7.5 hours	$ 144,000	$1,600
Provisors	7 hours	$ 288,000	$3,429
Total	54.5 hours	$1,152,000	$1,739 avg

These five activities will add $1,152,000 dollars over the next year. The average revenue per hour spent is $1,739 (this is skewed by the *great* return he gets from attending Provisor meetings around California).

Since Gordon was already complaining he was out of time, we were able to make some adjustments. We immediately cut the Quarterly In-Person events idea. With a return of only $800 per hour, it wasn't worth it. Those hours could be better spent either taking on more of one of the other activities—for instance, developing another new referral source per month—or directing those hours to another aspect of the firm to improve the way it operates. We don't know yet if these numbers will bear out, but we are tracking them and watching them, ready to make adjustments as the year progresses.

We spend a lot of time tracking the hours our firms devote to marketing because that is where the majority of clients come from in firms under $750,000. As you grow, you start to add paid sources such as Pay Per Click (PPC), paid referral sources, and snail-mail campaigns. Track these the same way—how much money did you spend on it, and how many dollars in revenue came back in? Find the average Return On Investment (ROI), and cut all activities that are below the average. It forces you, and any team members or consultants, to be very focused and judicious in the use of funds. As the average ROI rises, so will the income of your firm.

Key Number

While the most important number to nail down in this section is the Conversion Cycle, in and of itself, it isn't helpful. You need to know how many people are going in so you can know how many come out. The simplest number to use as your Key Number is the number of appointments booked. This quickly and easily tells you how many new clients you will have this month.

Keeping Score

How often do you look at it?

Check your Key Number (number of PNCs) each week.

Look at your Marketing KPIs at least once a month, more often for newer activities.

What does it tell you?

The Key Number tells you how many new cases you will have.

Your Conversion Rates show where you can improve both your sales process and marketing activities.

Give Yourself A Score

- If you track nothing, give yourself a 0.
- You may give yourself a 1 if you track the number of sales calls vs. the number of people who hire you.
- If you track all calls, the number of sales calls, the number of new clients, and revenue by referral source, you get a 2.
- Firms who track the full sales conversion cycle, revenue by referral source, and review all each month earn a 3.
- You get to give yourself a 4 if you track your full sales cycle, revenue by referral source, and how you are spending time and money on marketing each month.
- If you track every level of your sales cycle, all marketing activities in both time and dollars, track revenue by referral source, and look at these each month to see where you can make improvements, you earned yourself a 5.

On a scale of 0-5, my score is: _____

Why did you give yourself that score?

_____

_____

_____

_____

Results

Tracking your Marketing KPIs is an opportunity to make small adjustments to improve revenue, your bottom line, and your personal life. Gordon was able to make the decision about whether he would rather spend an extra five hours at home or spend it marketing because he knew exactly how much it would cost in revenue. By knowing where in your sales cycle your conversion rate is below average, you have the ability to make adjustments to become more efficient and waste less time. While Marketing KPIs are considered a more advanced "number," they give more stable law firm owners great insight into what is happening in their sales and marketing cycle.

How do conversion rates help you decide if you can stay on that beautiful desert island at the five-star resort? They are a predictor of your business. If you know your conversion rates, you can choose any number along the line, number of calls, number of appointments set, etc., and determine exactly how many cases will come in. We like appointments set as the Key Number. If you know how many appointments are set in the next week, you know whether or not you are needed at the office to help drive sales.

CHAPTER 7

CASE MANAGEMENT KPIs

Managing each employee's workload to ensure they are profitable, but not overworked, is a continual balancing act. To help, we use a few different Case Management KPIs. We talked about billable hour goals earlier. Each employee should have one and should be measured by this goal on a weekly basis. But there are other firmwide numbers that are equally important and essential when it comes to creating a profitable law firm.

Case Demographics

What does your average case look like? I know, I know—all your cases are different. However, if you start to look at what you do, you notice some things that are very helpful. The ones

> What does your average case look like?

that we like to know almost immediately are case make-up, average case value, and average case length. Let's use Martha's[43] firm as an example.

Martha is a divorce attorney in Florida who works almost exclusively with women. When we started working together, I needed

---

[43] Martha was my grandmother, and I have two cousins named after her—Martha Claire (who never uses the Martha part) and a young Martha who is less than 10 years old. Martha also happens to be my best friend's name. None of them are attorneys.

to be able to project numbers, but she didn't know much about her cases in terms of demographics. We sat down and divided her practice into a few buckets:

- Divorce with Children
- Divorce No Children
- Modifications
- Adoptions

By going into her case management system, we were able to determine what percentage of cases *(not revenue)* belonged to each bucket. Divorce with children was 50 percent, no children was 20 percent, modifications were 20 percent, and adoptions were 5 percent. The other 5 percent were random cases that didn't fit in the buckets. This was her case make-up.

Now that I knew Martha's case make-up, I needed the average case value and case length. We pulled ten random closed cases from each category,[44] noted the total billing amount, and the date opened and closed. After averaging those numbers, we knew case value and case length for each particular case type. A simple weighted average gave us one set of numbers for the firm as a whole.

In Martha's case, we discovered her average case value was $24,931, and cases lasted nine months.

---

[44] By the way, don't ever be the one to choose the cases. Let a member of your staff do it. I watch attorneys say, "Well, not this one because ..." and "You can't use that one ..." If you do this, we lose the random part. If you are very concerned about having an outlier, choose 12 cases and use the Olympic scoring method—throw out the highest and lowest and use the remaining ten.

Martha's Average Case Value		
Client Name[45]	Total Billed	Months Open
Roberts	$ 28,972	10
Kelly	$ 34,551	12
Morehead	$ 12,879	6
Schmid	$ 15,994	8
Whitaker	$ 41,857	13
Hendricks	$ 32,152	10
Russey	$ 18,366	14
Ryan	$ 25,142	8
Linker	$ 16,893	4
Wallace	$ 22,506	5
Average	$ 24,931	9

---

[45]   These are all last names of members of my family. Have I mentioned that my family is huge? And I am only talking about my mother's side in this book.

Cases per Team

The last piece of information we need to pull from those ten cases is how many hours were billed by paralegals, staff attorneys, and supervising attorneys. Using the same averaging method, we discover your firm's definition of a team for any particular case.

In Martha's case, it looked like this:

Job	Hours	Billing Rate	Billing Goal per Month
Paralegal	82	100	120 Hours
Staff Attorney	37	300	120 Hours
Supervising Attorney	14	375	60 Hours

Using this information, we could define Martha's team. Her Supervising Attorney wasn't the key person on a case. Instead, it was the staff attorney, so we based the team around this individual and came up with the following plan for what a team should look like when working on a case.

1 Staff Attorney

2.2 Paralegals (82/37)

.76 Supervising Attorney ($14 \div 37$) * 2[46]

All of a sudden, some things made sense. Martha's gut instinct had been validated. She now understood how many hours were required by each of her employees to work a case. From that point on, every staff attorney was assigned two paralegals. She also knew, as the supervising attorney, that if all she did was run her legal staff (no marketing, no

---

[46] The 2 is because the Supervising Attorney's goal is half that of the Staff Attorney.

office operations, just 30 hours of billing a week), she could manage 1.3 teams. And it let us know that when she thought she needed to hire a new team, she should start with a paralegal because that was the person on staff who would max out first.

How many cases could a team handle? Let's look at the staff attorney again. If she works 37 hours over 9 months, she works about 4.1 hours per month on a case. Her billing goal is 120, which means she can handle 120 ÷ 4.1 = about 29 cases at any given time. I know, I know—cases, especially ones where litigation is involved, aren't worked at a steady rate over the life of the case. However, you do have cases coming into the firm each month, which means there are cases at every stage on the docket, so the law of averages says this is a good number to use.

Total Cases and Net New Cases

As with many numbers, I like to look at the big one first. If anything seems amiss, then it's time to dig a little deeper. That is why I like tracking Total Cases. Knowing how many "teams" you have tells you how many cases you can handle. Aiming for this number and watching how it rises and falls tells us a lot about the way a firm is growing (or shrinking).

Let's go back to John, the attorney with the fast-growing firm in the Pacific Northwest. We tracked how many open cases he had by tracking cases opened and cases closed. Turns out, he was growing at the rate of five Net New Cases a month. This means that he opened five more cases than he closed in an average month. Using Martha's case demographics, that would mean he needs a new "team" about every seven and one-half to eight months. Wow. Wouldn't you like to know seven months before you need to hire somebody that you need them? Wouldn't that give you time to look for a great person instead of making what I call desperation hires?

Watching your Total Case count also alerts you to problems or major wins in your marketing and sales pipeline. When there is a big surge of new cases, find the marketing activity that caused it. If cases are dropping, what has changed? Has an ad quit working, or did you go on vacation and stop meeting with referral sources?

This was the case for Martha. She takes two weeks off every July (she is actually in Washington DC as I write this). The first year she took this time, it had a devastating effect on her business since she was the only person at her firm doing any kind of marketing and sales. As a result, the firm landed no new cases while she was away. We knew that would happen, but what was surprising was that Martha had a two-week dry spell of significantly fewer referrals a couple of weeks *after* she got back. It was horrible. We weren't prepared for her caseload to drop so drastically.

The next year, we planned more effectively. First, Martha taught other people in her office how to do a sales call. She started having her attorneys attend networking events and had them develop referral sources of their own. Finally, we stockpiled enough cash to get through any cash crunch that showed up in August. As Martha's firm has grown and she continues to implement and expand these measures, the impact of her leaving has lessened. This year, I doubt there will be any effect on her case count as a result of her time in DC.

Key Number

Of all the numbers we've discussed in this chapter, the Key Number got very little press, but it is very important. Net New Cases gives you a fast snapshot of what is happening in your firm. If the number is positive and about the same as, or larger than, other months, great. If it is negative, you should probably get on the supply

> Net New Cases gives you a fast snapshot of what is happening in your firm

boat because you have a cash crunch on the way. If you only get six numbers to make a decision, you want this to be one of them.

Keeping Score

How often do you look at it?

As the firm owner, you should look at your case counts on a monthly basis. Review average case value and length on a quarterly basis to check for trends. As new cases come into the firm, the person who assigns cases should look at the number of cases assigned to a staff attorney to determine which team needs more work.

What does it tell you?

All of these measures help you assess how much work is in your firm and when you need to hire or fire staff.

Give Yourself A Score

- If you track nothing, give yourself a 0.
- You may give yourself a 1 if you track the number of new cases and have an idea of average case value and length.
- Firms that track and review cases opened, cases closed, and total cases (by attorney) on a monthly basis earn a 2.
- If you track and review on a monthly basis all the case counts and have, at some point, done the research for case demographics (both average length and value), you get a 3.
- You get to give yourself a 4 if you complete all of the above plus you have determined the make-up of a "team."
- If you track opened and closed cases, total case count, plus revisit average case value, average case length, and review the definition of a team on a quarterly basis, you earn yourself a 5.

On a scale of 0-5, my score is: _____

Why did you give yourself that score?

_____

_____

_____

_____

Results

Confidently being able to predict the amount of work that will move through your office in the next month, three months, or even year is invaluable. The information provides important insights into knowing what staff you'll need to work those cases. You'll be able to look for and react to trends based on how quickly, or slowly, you are growing through your case count. Knowing these details allows you to get ahead of the curve, as John did when he was growing so rapidly. It also alerts you to problems, as we saw when Martha left town for two weeks. Most importantly, it allows you to adapt and make changes that will minimize (or maximize) the effects on your firm.

If I were sitting on an island and trying to decide whether I could stay longer, my Net New Case count would provide valuable information. If my Net New Case count was at zero, then next month would look pretty much like this month. If it was increasing by two or three cases, then things would be a little busier and probably on track with my plan. If it was increasing by ten, then I might need to head home to supervise the hiring that will need to be done. Conversely, if the Net New Cases count was negative, I would probably need to go home to work my contacts and perform other marketing activities to stimulate the business.

Whether the numbers are going up or down, knowing your Net New Case count lets you plan and adapt to changes.

CHAPTER 8

BALANCE SHEET

This book covers the 6 Key Numbers® that you need to know to run a profitable firm. Since I want to discuss one more, let's call this one a bonus number—the Balance Sheet. It is a basic yet very useful financial report, but I can't tell you how many people ignore or forget about this one. If your Budget versus Actual is a GPS to your year-end destination, your Balance Sheet is like a visit to the doctor for a checkup. Only in this case, you're checking the financial health of your firm.

What Is a Balance Sheet?

A Balance Sheet is divided into three sections:

Here's how they work together.

Assets – everything you own. This includes cash in the bank, any furniture or equipment in the office, and anything that is owed to you (loans you made), such as advanced client costs or employee advances. Unless your firm is over $5 million in revenue, you should be filing your taxes (and looking at all financial reports) on a cash basis. In this case, A/R should not show up on your Balance Sheet. If your firm is over $5 million and filing on an accrual basis, A/R will display as an asset. We always recommend that firms file and look at their financial reports on a cash basis as long as possible because that better reflects what is happening in your bank account.

Liabilities – everything you owe or borrowed. This includes your credit cards, line of credit, payroll taxes, car loan, outstanding bills, and any money you owe on furniture or equipment in your office.

Only one account shows up in both the Asset and Liability sections—your Trust or IOLTA account. As the name implies, the Trust account is money given to you by a client to hold in trust until it is either earned by you, needed by the client to pay another bill associated with their representation, or their case is completed, and it is returned to them. IT IS NOT YOUR MONEY. While it is deposited in an account with your firm name on it (Asset), the client has the right to demand it back at any time. For this reason, it also sits under Liabilities (things you owe).

Equity – the value of everything you own minus any debt, just like with your house. This is the book value of your law firm. If you were going to sell your firm today, this is the first place a buyer would look to start determining the price. The most notable account in this section is Shareholder Distribution.[47] This account records all cash draws, distributions, or payments made for personal expenses. The other important category is Net Income, which is the number the IRS uses to tax you.

Now that you understand how it works, here are some tips on how to use it. I like to look at what is called a Comparative Balance Sheet. A regular Balance Sheet is a snapshot in time. While useful, it gives you information in isolation. Just like we like to compare the P&L to your Profit Plan to give it context, I like to do the same with a Balance

---

[47] This account has lots of names. Others include Partner Distributions, Owner Distributions, and Profit Distributions. There are also all the same iterations except instead of distribution it may say draw.

Sheet. However, in the case of your Balance Sheet, I like to look at it over a period of time—YTD, six months, or even a year. To prepare this, simply have your bookkeeper run it with an appropriate time period and set the columns to Monthly. What you get is a chart that looks like the one on the next page.

A Comparative Balance Sheet shows you if you are making progress – or sliding backwards

	Jan 2019	Feb 2019	Mar 2019	Apr 2019
Dewey Cheatum and Howe, PLLC				
Balance Sheet				
As of April 30				
ASSETS				
Current Assets				
Bank Accounts				
10001 Citibank 5427	17,864	15,728	10,032	10,237
10002 Citibank 1358	33	4,718	923	0
10901 Citi Business Trust	303,764	317,575	315,409	321,290
Total Bank Accounts	$321,661	$338,021	$326,365	$331,528
Other Current Assets				
102 Advanced Client Costs	2,784	2,784	2,784	2,784
Total Other Current Assets	$2,784	$2,784	$2,784	$2,784
Total Current Assets	$324,445	$340,806	$329,149	$334,312
Fixed Assets				
151 Furniture and Equipment	18,051	18,051	18,051	18,051
153 Accumulated Depreciation	-6,715	-6,715	-6,715	-6,715
Total Fixed Assets	$11,336	$11,336	$11,336	$11,336
TOTAL ASSETS	$335,781	$352,141	$340,485	$345,648
LIABILITIES AND EQUITY				
Liabilities				
Current Liabilities				
200 Business AMEX 32003	2,365	2,880	2,368	818
220 Payroll Liabilities	6,187	6,355	6,173	7,623
250 Client Trust Liability	303,764	317,542	315,076	320,957
270 Line of Credit	26,472	21,472	20,000	18,000
Total Current Liabilities	$338,788	$348,249	$343,617	$347,398
Total Liabilities	$338,788	$348,249	$343,617	$347,398
Equity				
301 Partner Contributions	10,000	10,000	10,000	10,000
302 Partner Distribution	-15,267	-31,008	-45,988	-58,832
390 Retained Earnings	45,143	45,143	45,143	45,143
Net Income	14,053	67,918	80,353	117,717
Total Equity	$53,929	$92,053	$89,508	$114,029
TOTAL LIABILITIES AND EQUITY	$392,717	$440,302	$433,125	$461,427

From here, you start to see the progress of your company. Below is a checklist to help you "read" your Balance Sheet.

Assets

- **Is your bank account growing or shrinking?** Growing is good. Shrinking means that you will eventually run into cash crunches if you haven't already.

- **Is your Trust balance growing, and how many months of expenses are sitting in your Trust account?** This is a great judge of how much work is sitting in your account and can be an early indicator that you need to hire. Only you can determine the appropriate number of months for your firm, but we like three months and start to worry at five because you are starting a big backlog. If the balance is falling, it means you are either working the cases faster than you can refill the pipeline (assuming you are getting appropriate retainers and using evergreen clauses) and/or are overstaffed.

- **Are Advanced Client Costs growing?** If they are outpacing the growth rate of your revenue, it means that you are not collecting all the loans that you are making in the form of paying bills on behalf of your clients. Not all firms track their Advanced Client Costs on their Balance Sheet, but it is a best practice.

- **Do you have more Depreciation than Fixed Assets?** Your accountant uses depreciation every year to help you save on taxes. If you have depreciated your assets past zero, contact your accountant to fix the problem.

- **Negative is bad.** With the exception of Depreciation, all numbers should be positive. If they are negative, talk to your bookkeeper to see why. Unless you are in a major cash crunch and are overdrawn at the bank, negative balances are usually bookkeeping errors.

Liabilities

- **Are credit card and line of credit balances growing or shrinking?** Growing debt means that your firm (or you personally) is spending more than it is earning. It is easy to do, especially with credit cards, so be vigilant. Ultimately, there is only one type of debt we want to see—credit card balances showing only charges since the last statement that will be paid off before the next bill arrives.

- **Is the balance on Payroll Liabilities holding steady?** It is not uncommon to have some payroll liabilities on your balance sheet, depending upon when during the month your Balance Sheet is run. However, this number should not grow at a greater rate than your payroll itself. Not paying your payroll taxes is one of the things that really gets the attention of both the IRS and state agencies.

- **Does your Trust Liability equal your Trust Asset?** These two balances should always match. If they don't, contact your bookkeeper immediately since this is one of the leading reasons attorneys are disciplined by the Bar Association.

- **Is your Trust Liability listed by client?** Many firms like to see their Trust Liability by client on the Balance Sheet. While not necessary, you should be able to drill down on the Liability number to find each individual's balance and a list of their transactions. This is used to do a three (3) way reconciliation between your accounting software, practice management software, and the bank.

- **Again, negative balances are bad.** All balances should be positive. This is most crucial with your Trust accounts since a negative balance means you have spent client money or recorded a transaction improperly.

Assets

- **Shareholder Contributions should be steady.** Unless you have a new partner buying in, this number should remain steady. If it is growing, the firm is typically spending more money than it is generating, and the partners are paying in to keep it afloat.

- **Is the balance of the Shareholder Draw account accurate?** This is the money that you have taken home this year in the form of draws and distributions. Does it look about right, or does it say you have removed $5,000,000? One of the most typical errors we see on a balance sheet is that the tax accountant does not send year-end journal entries to the bookkeeper. Your balance as of January 1 should be zero. The adjustment is made retroactively as soon as taxes are filed.

- **Are Shareholder Draws greater than Net Income?** As a business owner, it becomes so easy to take money out of the firm when it is sitting in the business account. However, if you are taking out more in Draws that the firm is making in Net Income, then you are starving the firm of cash and racking up company debt to fund your personal lifestyle. Stop! Find ways to save money at home, and you should start to see the difference between these two numbers shrinking. Financially healthy firms have Shareholder Draws that are less than Net Income.

- **The only account that should be negative is Shareholder Distributions.** This is money you took out of the firm, so it shows as a withdrawal. When your Total Equity number is negative, it means that your firm is Technically Insolvent. This is not the end of the world and does not mean you should close the firm or declare bankruptcy. It simply means you have borrowed more money than you can pay back today. Take a look at how you are spending money both at the firm and at home and make the cuts necessary to reverse the situation.

Key Number

The Key Number is the whole Balance Sheet. Your Balance Sheet is a scorecard that illustrates your financial position. Use it to keep score and keep you on track.

Keeping Score

How often do you look at it?

Check your Balance Sheet no less than every other month, though I check mine every month.

What does it tell you?

How financially healthy your firm is and, when using a Comparative Balance Sheet, if you are becoming sicker or more valuable.

Give Yourself A Score

- If your bookkeeper doesn't produce a Monthly Balance Sheet, give yourself a 0.

- You may give yourself a 1 if you get a Balance Sheet every month, but it has negative numbers, or your Trust Asset and Liability don't match.

- If your bookkeeper produces an accurate report without any year-end Journal Entries, but you never look at it, you get a 2.

- Firms who read the report each month but do little with it earn a 3.

- You get to give yourself a 4 if you review the Balance Sheet each month, but it only covers one point in time (usually the last day of the month).

- If your bookkeeper produces a Comparative Balance Sheet with no negative numbers (except Draws) that you review to look for progress, you have earned yourself a 5.

On a scale of 0-5, my score is: _____

Why did you give yourself that score?

_____

_____

_____

_____

Results

The Balance Sheet is an opportunity to see quickly whether your firm is healthy and its overall trajectory. It is easy to look at improving revenue and forget that there is more to it. It is also easy to lose sight of how much you are spending both at the office and at home.

Your Balance Sheet never lies. It shows you if you are taking on more debt or climbing out of the hole. It is usually the most enlightening report for firms that are growing fast. We have noticed over the past few years, that the faster a firm grows, the faster the owner's lifestyle and personal cash needs also grow. The firms tend to face numerous cash crunches, which the owners blame on growth—without realizing they are a main cause. When we show clients that they are removing (and spending) more than the firm is making, they start to understand.

Are you making progress or slipping backward? Owners who are moving forward can feel confident that they can stay on the island for another week. Firms that are moving backward (incurring more debt, Trust balance shrinking) will need to get off the island and get back to the office.

CHAPTER 9

WHY DOES IT MATTER?

I started this book telling you about Patricia and how she felt her firm was out of control and stressful. She didn't even know if she was running a viable business. By working through the 6 Key Numbers®, she was able to create not only a business she loved but one which allowed her to live the life she wanted to live (not to mention sleep soundly at night).

Cash. The first thing we did was get a handle on her cash. How much did she have, and how much was coming in? We then controlled the timing of when she got paid and projected the amount of money she would have at the end of every week for the next six to eight weeks. Knowing she was going to get paid for the work she did, knowing in advance how much cash she would have, and knowing if there was going to be a cash crunch made her a much more confident when making decisions.

Ideal Ratios. By introducing Patricia to the Key Ratios, we finally got her firm balanced and paying her what she deserved. This alleviated stress both at the office and at home. At work, it enabled her to be more confident when creating profitable compensation plans. She knew whether or not she should embark on a new marketing campaign. At home, it allowed her to *know* how much cash she would get every month. Bills were consistently paid, and personal cash crunches eliminated.

Producing Legal Services. Once each of Patricia's employees had billing goals to which they were held accountable, revenue immediately rose. The fact that it allowed her to predict what would happen in the future was almost a bonus! Understanding how much work could move through her firm, how much of that capacity she was using, and knowing when she would run out of capacity started informing her hiring decisions. Looking at her billable people as inventory allowed Patricia to step back from the emotion of running her firm and make data-based decisions.

Budget vs. Actual. When we started the Profit Planning process, Patricia moved from nightmares about her firm to dreams about the future. What did she want? How long would it take her to achieve those things? By allowing herself to dream and putting a plan to it, she realized she could accomplish much more in a year than she had ever thought possible. She now enjoys reviewing her Budget vs. Actual as it gives her a chance to get back on track or repeat profitable activities and measure her progress. Her dreams are coming true.

Marketing and Sales. Marketing and sales had been a mystery for Patricia. Clients came to her, though she didn't really know how or why. Some hired her, and some didn't. Once she started tracking her activities and those of potential clients, she understood the process. She was able to change the way she spoke to referral sources about her firm, which resulted in better referrals. She evaluates her marketing activities and cuts out ones where the ROI is too low, freeing up time to bill more or spend time with her family.

Case Management KPIs. When we first started talking about the demographics of her cases, Patricia saw very little value. Now she understands that shortening a case results in a happier client (more referrals). She understands what the make-up of her team should be and how many cases the team can handle. By tracking her Net New Cases, she is easily able to predict when she will need to hire new staff. In the past, she would get overworked and make desperation hires who later sucked up a bunch of time as she tried to train them to be the employee she wanted, before ultimately firing them. Now, she has the luxury of time to start her search early enough and hire only "A" players for her team. This has improved the culture and teamwork of her firm—opening up untold hours that were previously spent dealing with HR issues.

Balance Sheet. By using all the other "numbers," Patricia can see the financial stability of her firm on her Balance Sheet. Her debt is dropping, her cash is rising, and she is taking less out of the firm than it is earning. She is no longer technically insolvent. In fact, according to her balance sheet, she looks very attractive to potential buyers. But being bought out isn't what Patricia wants. Why would she? She is currently on a desert island at a five-star resort picking up a little piece of paper with 6 Key Numbers on it so she can make a decision about staying.

- **Cash Flow Forecast** – she has plenty of cash for the next eight weeks. No problems there.

- **Owner Compensation** – she is still making what she should be. She can pay for another week at the resort.

- **WIP** – her people are all billing to their goals, and at this point, there is more WIP than she will have in expenses next month. Check!

- **Budget vs. Actual** – Patricia is on track to meet her goals, and there are no red flags that need her attention. That is a green light for staying.

- **Number of new PNCs** – she likes to have eight per month, and she has twelve scheduled, so her firm is golden.

- **Net New Cases** – this is six, and her monthly goal is five, which means she is in the clear.

Patricia gets a small grin on her face, hands the captain the piece of paper back, and turns to the front desk person helping departing guests onto the boat, "I'll be staying for another week."

But what about you? Add up the scores you gave yourself in each section:

Cash Flow Forecast   _____

Owner Compensation   _____

Work In Progress   _____

Budget vs. Actual   _____

Scheduled Sales Calls   _____

Net New Cases   _____

Total   _____

If your score is less than 14, you identify closely with Panicked Patricia and have some serious work ahead of you. A score between 15 and 25 means you have some idea of what is happening, but there are holes that can still cause anxiety. If your score is 26+, you are standing on the beach next to Profitable Patricia with a huge smile on your face.

CHAPTER 10

HOW TO

There are people in the legal industry who like to understand exactly how things are done and/or feel like they can't afford to outsource tasks. This section is for all the DIYers who want to go deeper into how to execute some of the things I've discussed in the book. The How To section covers:

- How to write a fee agreement that gets you paid
- How to use a fee agreement to get paid (these are different— one is about how to write the document while the second details how to use the document)
- How to get your books done
- How to create a Cash Flow Forecast
- How to create a Profit Plan

As you found throughout the book, additional stories and downloads are available at CathCap.com. The How To section and the additional online information should make the concepts discussed easier to understand and apply.

How to: Write a Fee Agreement That Gets You Paid

A/R is a constant conversation, but the big question is, what should you do to fix it? What changes can you make right now to improve A/R and your bottom line? The first step towards improving A/R involves fixing the problem before it occurs. From the initial client meeting, a firm needs to set clear expectations and explain the consequences. The A/R policy should be communicated during the first meeting with every potential new client. When this doesn't occur, policies and procedures that are weak, nonexistent, or not followed can quickly become standard. Firms need to set the proper expectations not only with their clients but also within their firm.

When we start working with a new client, we immediately look at existing policies and procedures to determine how (if at all) expectations are being set with the client and within the firm. We also suggest they call late-paying clients and follow that up with demand letters, but the priority when moving forward is to create a clear A/R structure that avoids late payments.

Since the fee agreement is where expectations are set, we'll start there. By reworking a few sections, firms can create structures that almost completely eradicate A/R going forward.[48]

Set Client Payment Expectations

A fee agreement sets expectations by detailing how the client-attorney relationship will work and by establishing parameters. It's the perfect place to add wording about how and when you get paid. Simply put, this is where you tell clients that you are going to be paid—on time and every month. I worked with an attorney named Lucy,[49] who had a

---

[48]   If you don't have a fee agreement, get one. Every state suggests you use them, and many require it. If you haven't drafted one, most State Bars have one that you can download for free.

[49]   Lucy is a cousin and also one of my closest friends. She can always be counted on to make you laugh and forget anything bad in your life.

paragraph in her fee agreement talking about nonpayment that went into great detail about setting up payment plans or taking a lien on a piece of property to get paid (later).

I immediately cut that paragraph. She was basically telling new clients that they didn't have to pay her and that she would bend over backward to do everything she could to make it as easy as possible for them not to pay her. Lucy is a tax attorney. Her clients have already proven they are happy *not* to pay bills. She knows they don't like to pay bills because it is why they had to hire her in the first place—to fix their nonpayment of taxes. With that in mind, any possible nonpayment loopholes needed to be closed.

We explained to Lucy why that paragraph was damaging and why we eliminated it. In just six weeks, her collection rate went up four percent. For a firm earning $1.5 million, that translates to $60,000 a year. And that was just in the first six weeks. She had not even had all of her clients sign the new fee agreement yet!

When entering a new client relationship, it is imperative that expectations are clear. Don't undercut your own credibility by giving them nonpayment options. You are going to represent a client, and they are going to pay you for said representation. Make sure this correlation is acknowledged and understood.

Withdrawal for Nonpayment

Another important part of a fee agreement involves adding language that allows a firm to stop representing clients who don't pay. We suggested that Lucy add this to her fee agreement to provide an easier exit from cases where clients are not paying. In the legal field, it's difficult to stop representing a client during the legal process, even if they're not paying you. There are only a few ways to get out—win the case, lose the case; withdraw from the case, or get fired.

Winning or losing means you complete the case. Withdrawing can be problematic. Even though many states allow attorneys to withdraw if a client is not paying, getting a judge to agree to that can be difficult. However, if you get fired, a judge must let an attorney out of a case.

With that understanding, and after reviewing hundreds of fee agreements and learning more about the specific Bar Rules of each state, we suggest that an automatic firing clause be included in every client's fee agreement. Basically, this addition states that if a client misses a certain number of payments, then they have essentially fired your firm.

Here is an example of what that might look like in legalese:

If Client fails to make three payments in a row, then Client has voluntarily terminated the relationship with the Firm, and arrangements will be made to return any materials and remaining money held in trust as soon as possible.[50]

Lucy lives in a state where a firing clause is permissible. After adding it to her fee agreement, she told us, "That was worth every penny I paid you—just for that one sentence." When this clause is activated, it should then be backed up with a signed Motion to Withdraw, stating that the client has terminated representation.[51] Sometimes just the threat of activating this clause is enough to get a client to pay. If not, be careful to manage the relationship with the departing client—you don't want them bad-mouthing you all over town.

Retainers

The next element every firm should detail in the fee agreement relates to the management of retainers. Some firms get a token

---

[50] Check your Bar rules. Not every state allows this.

[51] Again, check your Bar Rules. Remember, I am not an attorney, nor am I giving legal advice here. I'm just sharing what has worked for hundreds of clients over the years. It is your responsibility to read the Rules. Have I said I'm not engaging in the unauthorized practice of law? I'm not. I promise. Just sharing my experiences.

amount or whatever they feel the client can afford, and this is a huge mistake. All retainers should cover *at least* the first three months of anticipated billing.

Why three months? That's an easy answer—to cover your costs. Think about a typical billing cycle. You are hired on September 5th and start working immediately. On October 1st, you send out a bill. No matter what that bill says, most clients feel they have 30 days to pay. You continue working their case all through October and, on November 1st, send out the next bill. At this point, firms generally start trying nicely to collect because the client is now past due. But work doesn't stop on their case. All through the month of November, you are working the case, and you bill for those hours on December 1st.

The client hasn't paid you a penny, and they are just now 30 days past due, so your collection efforts really ramp up. Basically, it takes about three months to determine whether your client is going to pay on time or not. Always get three months up-front, so you are covered in the event you were hired by a deadbeat, or somebody going through financial difficulties they failed to reveal at the time they hired you. Either way, it affects your ability to represent them and your ability to get compensated for your time.

Evergreen Retainer

The other change we make to the retainer involves adding what is commonly referred to as an evergreen clause. This ensures that a certain amount of money remains in the client's trust account at all times. If the level dips below that predetermined amount, then the client needs to send in money to make up the difference. Think of the evergreen retainer as an insurance policy for you. It guarantees that you have access to payment at all times. By incorporating this element into the fee agreement, you've formalized the payment process with a structured and clearly stated plan. You can see how this protects you from nonpayment and its ensuing troubles.

Here's how it works. Your agreement states that while an initial retainer of $XXX is due at the time the fee agreement is executed, a minimum of $YYY must remain in the client's trust account at all times. Guess how much $YYY is. Yup, about three months. However, since most cases bill heavier in the first few months, the evergreen amount is usually less than the initial retainer.

I have been asked why it is even necessary to have an evergreen amount when a client has proven that they will pay by providing the retainer amount. I can think of many reasons, but my top two reasons should be persuasive enough. First, clients can (and will) stop paying at any time for any reason. Why they stop paying usually has little to do with the attorney or the case and is more about some other aspect of their life. Second, the longer a case goes on, the less likely the client will be able to afford your bills. In this scenario, the evergreen amount insulates you and enables you to complete the case, or at least make alternate payment arrangements.

When we discuss these changes to retainers, many owners are interested in the outcomes but concerned about overseeing the process. They fear that adding in evergreen retainers will complicate an already complicated element of their business. On the one hand, this is true. Account levels will need to be monitored more closely, so additional evergreen payment amounts are triggered and to ensure that clients pay the correct amounts. Many firm management software packages have this feature built-in. But considering the alternative, we've found that the additional effort is financially worth it since it exponentially increases your collection amount.

In fact, it helps you completely bypass the standard billing cycle pattern of billing, waiting, waiting, waiting, and (hopefully) depositing. I am constantly amazed at the way people pay their bills, and it's a process you likely want to work around, if possible.

My best friend, Lauren,[52] is a great example of the vagaries of billing. She is extraordinarily successful. Lauren is head of communications at a Fortune 500 company where she manages an enormous budget with a staggering number of employees. But, opening mail is not her strength. I was visiting her last year, and while we were chatting, she opened a drawer that was *stuffed* with envelopes. She took them out and started opening.

Lauren admitted to me that she hadn't opened mail in six weeks. All of her regularly occurring bills are on autopay, so most of what arrives at her house is junk mail. About every six weeks, she goes through it and, inevitably, finds a couple of one-off bills. Attorneys are almost always one-off bills. This is what you are up against if you are working with clients who are hiring you as individuals. By the way, after opening, she put the bills back in the drawer to pay another day.

If your clients are companies, it is only marginally better. You send a bill on the 1st, and it gets opened and put in the pile to be paid with the next round of checks since most companies pay bills twice a month. At the first set of check writing, your bill probably won't be paid because most clients think they have until the end of the month before it is due. At the second round of bill paying, the client's bookkeeper prioritizes the bills, adds them up, determines how much money they have, and then pays the ones they can afford. How high up do you think the legal bill is? Not very. Their lawyer isn't going to send letters or call at all hours of the day and night, like most bill collectors. They won't shut off the electricity, TV, or water like the utility companies will. And experience has taught them that their attorney will not withdraw from the case. There is very little downside for them for not paying the bill.

---

[52] Using my sister's name here, which is a shame because I am incredibly proud of what my best friend has accomplished in her career, and this makes her look like a flake. On the other hand, my sister is one of the most disciplined people I have ever encountered, and she would never let this happen in her household. Oh well, my sister can get all the glory on this one.

By having money in trust throughout the case, it is more likely that you will get paid. It is more likely that you and your staff will spend less time trying to collect money. And it is more likely that you will take home more money as the owner.

Credit Cards

My final solution to guarantee prompt bill payment is simple—take the timing of payments out of the clients' hands. You should be in control of when and how you get paid. Sounds ideal, right? To make this happen, we suggest adding a few sentences to the fee agreement saying that once an invoice has been sent out, the client has XX number of days (we usually use 10) to either pay the invoice or dispute the charges.[53] If they do neither, the firm will move money from the IOLTA account to pay the invoice and will then charge their credit card to keep their trust account balance in compliance with the fee agreement.

I just heard a whole lot of people groan because they think paying three percent to a credit card company is a waste of money. Those people are wrong. Here is what happens when you accept credit cards:

- You can determine the timing of when you get paid.
- You get paid faster.
- You are better able to predict your cash on hand.
- You are more likely to get paid since the client can't prioritize other bills in front of yours.
- Your A/R drops dramatically.

This is a win-win situation. Yes, the client wins in this transaction, too. Not only do they get to collect miles or cashback from their credit

---

[53] Each state Bar has different rules on how many days you must wait before moving money from Trust or charging a client's card. Please check your state's Bar Rules before implementing this process.

card, but it is one less bill they need to pay and one less headache to worry about.

To make all of this work, you need the client to authorize you to charge their card. This is a two part-er. First, we add a sentence in the body of the fee agreement saying that we can charge their card to keep them in compliance with the fee agreement. Then, we place a form at the end of their fee agreement with language saying they authorize you to charge the card (the form includes spaces for the last four digits of the card, expiration date, CID code, billing address, and a credit card authorization specific signature).

You lawyers are still groaning—this time about the amount of work all of this takes. There is good news. Much of this can be automated. Keep reading—I have outlined everything you need to know in the next section.

How to: Use a Fee Agreement to Get Paid

After revising your fee agreement, it's likely that you'll need to increase your initial retainer amount. If you were charging one, it was probably too low and didn't cover the first three months of billing. Not surprisingly, at this point, my team and I get a lot of pushback from owners saying that the clients can't afford to pay that much. That may or may not be true. Remember one of the definitions of A/R from an earlier chapter? I compared it to an unsecured loan at zero percent interest to your clients. Is this a service you want to offer your clients? If not, then let's figure out how to help clients pay you.

Potential clients come to see you at their maximum point of pain.[54] They need your expertise and can't stand whatever their issue is anymore. As proof, they have actually resorted to hiring an attorney—not most lay peoples' idea of a fun day. By the time they leave your office after hiring you, they took the problem that was keeping them up at night and dumped it on your desk. They leave much happier.

Keep this in mind. Clients are most motivated to pay you at the point of maximum pain. They are at their most resourceful when their problem is interfering with their lives. If your client is not motivated enough to pay you a retainer at this moment, what are the chances that they are going to pay you when they're *not* in pain? Pretty low.

Help your client find the money. Ask them if they have a relative who can help them pay, if they can go to their bank to get a loan, if they have room on their credit cards, or if they can get cash anywhere else. If the answer is no, you need to think long and hard about whether you want this client. There are a number of places where our clients send their clients to get loans for legal bills. All have applications online, and most give a thumbs up or thumbs down immediately. Funding happens within hours and days. If you want to access the list we give our clients, go to CathCap.com/PanictoProfitResources.

---

[54]   I love this phrase—maximum point of pain. I learned it from Lucy, the tax attorney in New York.

If your potential client can't get a loan to pay for your services, you really don't need that client. I promise that companies who loan money for a living are much better at determining the creditworthiness of a client than you are. And if a client's family won't loan them money, well, they have insider info that you haven't discovered yet. Basically, if someone can't finance your services from the start, RUN. They are not a client you want, and you will end up financing it, to the horror of your spouse and bank account. Don't do it. Okay, that's the end of my rant.

Working with higher caliber clients (ones that pay) improves the experience for everybody in your firm, and most importantly, for your team. Clients that pay also tend to communicate more effectively with their attorney. They are more likely to respond quickly to requests for information. They are easier to work with. In short, they become part of the "team." While it might feel scary and seem like you are losing business in the beginning, remember that if you were only collecting 75 percent of what you were owed, by raising your collection rate, you can lose 25 percent of your client base and still make the same amount of money. Weed out potential deadbeats and watch the morale of your firm soar—not to mention the profit going in your pocket.

New Collection Process

Once we implement these changes, you've successfully created a clear system and foundation for collecting payment. By incorporating it into the fee agreement, your expectations are communicated to clients from the first meeting. There should be no debate or confusion. Better yet, once the system is up and running, many aspects of it can be fully automated.

Here's what the new and improved payment process looks like:

- Client signs fee agreement.
- Initial charge for retainer is processed (or check deposited).

- Invoice is sent to client at end of billing period.

- If there is more money in trust than the evergreen retainer requires, move money into the operating account after XX days.[55] In most cases, 10 days complies with Bar rules.

- If the IOLTA balance is at the evergreen level, charge the card and deposit invoiced amount directly into the operating account.

- If a card is declined, contact client.

- If they do not comply with the fee agreement within 4–6 weeks, stop work on the file.

- If they do not pay within three months, trigger the firing clause.

Much of this process can be automated. We always recommend that our clients use LawPay as their processing company. They are payment management specialists who have a thorough understanding of the legal industry. LawPay provides firms with the flexibility to deposit funds into *either* an operating or trust account. They're familiar with compliance issues around IOLTA accounts, and they process both credit card and ACH Debit payments.

Because they are a leading provider of payment management services, they have worked hard to integrate their software with many different legal software providers. LawPay and Clio just rolled out a new integration that automates payments. Clio now automatically initiates evergreen replenishments and credit card charges. Similarly, Rocket Matter, a cloud-based legal management software, offers its own credit card processing service called Rocket Matter Payments that is included with every subscription. With a little set-up, charging every client is as easy as hitting the "go" button. All of the above becomes automatic—even charging the credit cards to bring the evergreen balances into

---

[55]   Again, check your state's Bar rules to make sure you are giving the client enough notice. Still not practicing law.

compliance! That particular feature saved one of our clients two entire days a month of inputting and charging credit cards.

Some software integrates but only pushes information to LawPay. When you use Practice Panther, you can initiate all charges from within Panther. Panther will also automatically move money from trust, create a report about what was moved, and let you know which accounts have balances that have dropped below the evergreen amount. And all of that information is reflected on the next invoice. All you have to do is go online with your bank and make one lump transfer.

Always leverage technology whenever you can to eliminate human error, human time, and the ability of a human to avoid doing something. Once properly set up, the system will only need monitoring from the partner (you). Set-up can seem like a daunting task, and if you don't know what you are doing and are not technologically savvy, it can be. After watching numerous clients struggle with this, we finally started a new business unit that does nothing but integrations. If you feel overwhelmed by setting up the procedures and integrations that make the collection process work seamlessly, don't hesitate to reach out to a professional to have them do it for you. We promise they will be able to do it faster, better, and cheaper than you can.

How to: Get Your Books Done

When starting a firm, attorneys wear all kinds of hats. They are the paralegal, associate, rainmaker, bookkeeper, office manager, and sometimes even the receptionist. As the firm grows, you get to shed some of those roles that are not the highest and best use of your time. The first to go is receptionist, quickly followed by paralegal, and then office manager. The role that attorneys most like to, well, dump is bookkeeper. Very few lawyers have a background in accounting, so there is little joy in keeping the books. As soon as they feel like they can "afford" a bookkeeper, they hire one.

You are right. Doing your books isn't the highest and best use of your time. But before you off-load this responsibility, make sure you have a good framework set up that will allow you, the bookkeeper, key employees, and even your tax accountant to access the information each of you needs to run the firm efficiently and profitably.

Technology is a beautiful thing that allows all these people to be involved, have the information they need (and nothing beyond that), and help you make smart decisions. Make sure you choose firm management software that is integrated (or at least syncs) with your bookkeeping software and then make relevant parts of it available to each party.

There are lots of ways to manage your finances, but the most important thing is to manage them. A number of things can happen when you don't monitor and track your bottom line. We have all heard horror stories of attorneys who have hired bookkeepers with the idea that they will no longer have to think about finances, only to have their accounts emptied, and they are left with a mess.

Because of this, we meet a lot of lawyers who do their own books. But here's an observation: attorneys are horrible bookkeepers! You went to law school because they promised you no numbers. And that's okay. We don't all have to be experts in everything. In order to protect themselves from theft, they swing a little far to one side and do their own accounting. Since this isn't their area of expertise, it can backfire and actually erode profits.

It brings to mind an attorney we worked with in Chicago. Michael[56] was a great guy. His practice was doing over a million dollars a year in healthcare law, but he didn't keep any books. Instead, he kept all his financial information in his head. Every year he closed his firm the week between Christmas and New Year's. Instead of enjoying this time with his wife and children, he holed up in his basement home office and put every single transaction from the whole year into QuickBooks. His books ended up being just a regurgitation of his bank statements. They couldn't be used to help him plan or make any kind of decisions. And who can remember what that $800 purchase was for in February?

Michael didn't want to hire a bookkeeper because he was afraid of theft. He was also apprehensive about taking on another cost. Who could blame him? He never had more than a rough idea of how much money he had in the bank! I know for a fact that his wife felt it would be more profitable for him to hire somebody to do this on a monthly basis, so they knew how much money they had, and so he could spend an entire week having family time.

When Cathedral Capital started working with him, we immediately had him hire a bookkeeper. In the past, on January 1st, he had beautiful and accurate books, but they wouldn't get updated for another whole year. This time, he hired a bookkeeper at the beginning of the year, turned over the beautiful books, and she updated them. Every month. Like clockwork. He could log into his QuickBooks Online at any time and see what his true cash balance was. Michael was amazed at the sense of security it gave him, and his wife and children were probably ecstatic that Dad now had an additional week of vacation to spend with them.

---

56   Michael is yet another cousin who is an attorney. He practices in Mississippi, and I promise you, his wife Monique is not letting him do something as foolish as this client was doing.

Even firms that have bookkeepers on staff to handle daily operations need to stay involved in the process. We worked with another firm in Texas that swung in the opposite direction from Michael. The owner, Shannon,[57] didn't delegate the responsibility for her books to a bookkeeper, she abdicated it. When she brought us on, we discovered that the bookkeeper hadn't reconciled the books in about six months. Payroll was being recorded but incorrectly. Deposits weren't being recorded at all. And, well, let's just say her books said she was $233,000 OVERDRAWN!

Shannon never checked the books to verify what her bookkeeper was doing. When we discovered the bookkeepers' activities (or lack thereof), we had a tough conversation with Shannon about what was going on. Once she understood that her bookkeeper had not been doing her job, she had two options: ignore the problem or take control and face the challenge head-on. Luckily, she chose option two.

She needed a new approach to managing her books, so we started at the beginning. Among other things, we taught her the importance of having an accurate cash balance, gave her some rudimentary knowledge of QuickBooks so she would understand what was happening, and recommended she fire the bookkeeper. We found that she had $17,000 of earned income in her trust account that she could transfer immediately. Shannon found a new bookkeeper and was ready to start fresh and stay involved in the process.

None of this was easy. In fact, it was all pretty scary. After the new bookkeeper started, Shannon wrote to me and said, "It has been challenging, daunting, and painful. But we grow through the cracks, don't we?"

---

[57]   Shannon is Michael's real life sister, though not an attorney.

How to: Create a Cash Flow Forecast

Unfortunately, this is not a report that you can pull from your firm management software or from your bookkeeping software. It is an old-school Excel spreadsheet, though it is easy to create.[58]

Here are some quick instructions:

- Pick a day to complete the CFF (I like to start them on Monday morning) and put each subsequent date in the cell to the right until you go out at least six weeks.

- On the first line, put your Cash Balance. It will be empty to the right for now.

- Below it, add the amount you are going to collect based on billing. If you aren't going to charge credit cards this week, then put the amount you will charge (based on your WIP) in the appropriate week. If you aren't charging cards, take your Billing Grid[59] and divide the total billing by 52 weeks and put that amount in each cell on that row.

- On the next line, if you have any clients that you know are going to pay you money they owe, put that in the appropriate week with a note saying who and how much.

- Now add up the columns—this is the cash you have to spend.

- Below that create a few categories:

  - Payroll – put the total amount deducted from your account in specific weeks.

  - Recurring bills – you know what you have to pay and when. Program that out.

- Credit Card – if you are like most of our clients, you put almost everything on your credit card to maximize points or cash back. In the week it is due, put the amount you usually pay.
- Extraordinary expenses – things come up. A new employee requires a new computer, or there is a one-time charge for something. These expenses go on this line along with a note about what it is and how much it cost.
- Total the expense categories, and this is how much you anticipate you will spend each week.
- Subtract the expenses from the revenue number, and you have your ending balance.
- At the top of the spreadsheet, make the beginning balance equal the ending balance from the previous week.

Here are some things you need to realize:

- It is going to be wrong for the first few weeks. That's okay. It gets more accurate the longer you use it.
- This is an ESTIMATE. It will never be totally accurate. That's okay, too.
- At the end of the week, put in the actual balance in that bottom cell. This will reset everything going forward.
- If the difference between your anticipated balance and actual balance is big, look into it. You don't need to find every penny, but if possible, make adjustments going forward. If it is small, blow it off.

Cash Flow Forecast

CATHEDRAL CAPITAL

Week Beginning	6-Apr	13-Apr	20-Apr	27-Apr	4-May	11-May	18-May	25-May	1-Jun	8-Jun
Beginning Balance:	23,497.00	54,009.00	45,904.00	39,099.00	91,214.00	94,761.00	89,936.00	78,941.00	75,694.00	45,808.00
Trust Transfers	37,500.00				37,500.00					37,500.00
A/R		5,000.00						2,500.00		
Contingency Cases				72,500.00						
Expenses										
Payroll*	(2,754.00)	(9,425.00)	(2,754.00)		(12,179.00)		(9,425.00)	(2,754.00)	(9,425.00)	(2,754.00)
Regular Expenses	(4,034.00)	(980.00)	(3,851.00)	(15,185.00)	(2,824.00)	(2,125.00)	(1,370.00)	(2,793.00)	(15,261.00)	(4,021.00)
Owner Draw		(2,500.00)		(5,000.00)		(2,500.00)			(5,000.00)	
Extraordinary Expenses					(14,500.00)					
Business Savings	(200.00)	(200.00)	(200.00)	(200.00)	(200.00)	(200.00)	(200.00)	(200.00)	(200.00)	(200.00)
LOC Drawdown/Payback					(4,250.00)					
Anticipated Balance	54,009.00	45,904.00	39,099.00	91,214.00	94,761.00	89,936.00	78,941.00	75,694.00	45,808.00	76,333.00
Actual Balance										
Cash Available	75,334.00	67,429.00	60,824.00	113,139.00	121,136.00	116,511.00	105,716.00	102,669.00	72,983.00	103,708.00
Business Savings Balance	575.00	775.00	975.00	1,175.00	1,375.00	1,575.00	1,775.00	1,975.00	2,175.00	2,375.00
LOC Balance	4,250.00	4,250.00	4,250.00	4,250.00	0.00	0.00	0.00	0.00	0.00	0.00

LOC Limit	$ 25,000.00

How to: Create a Profit Plan

A Profit Plan builds on some of the numbers we have already discussed. You already know how much you should be spending and where (this was in the Key Ratios section). Let's look at how you build a Profit Plan. There is no "right" way, and different people start different places. But since we consistently use the 6 Key Numbers®, we are a little more methodical than most people. So, let's open an Excel spreadsheet and get to work. Down the left side, we are going to write all the ways we make and spend money. Across the top, put the months of the year. Later in the process, we will start to fill in the numbers that correspond to the story.

Step 1: Revenue

We like starting with revenue since there is nothing worse than getting all your expenses built out and thinking, "Oh my gosh—I am never going to be able to cover all those expenses." By starting with revenue, our clients never have that "Oh s*&t" moment.

You can project your revenue in a few different ways. The first is the way your bookkeeper would probably do it. She (or he) would run the Budget Wizard in QuickBooks, and it would automatically plug in the revenue you had for this year into next year's budget. This assumes everything next year will be exactly like this year. That is pretty unrealistic, so not our favorite method.

The second way to project revenue would be the way your accountant would probably do it—by looking at your trend. If your revenue has been rising by three percent a year, every year, for the past five years, then many people would suggest simply projecting out a three percent increase. If you are happy with what has been happening in your firm, then, by all means, do this. Generally, our clients are not satisfied with such a small increase.

We recommend a two-step method. The first step projects revenue based on your capacity. You can take your billing grid and plug-in those numbers for revenue.

Then, you need to layer the second step on top. This is where the story of your firm comes into play. What are your dreams? Do you want to hit $1 million in revenue? Ten million? Do you want to add people—a new attorney or a couple of paralegals? Looking at your billing grid, add the people you want when you think you will be ready for them until you hit your revenue goals. Or, simply add the people you want and see where your revenue ends up.

Remember, it is unrealistic to think that a new employee will start and hit their billing goal in the first month. First, you may not have enough work to fill their time completely. Second, they will need to learn the way your firm does things, which slows billing. And third, they'll need to get caught up on the cases themselves, so you will be covering some of their time. We recommend giving billable employees three months to ramp up to their billing goals.

If you would like to download a billing grid to make this a little easier, go to CathCap.com/PanictoProfitResources.

Many attorneys don't look at their revenues based on billable hours. They like to project them based on marketing and the number of cases their sales funnel can bring in every month. Both methods are valid. It depends on how you like to look at things. Sometimes it is helpful to do it both ways to double-check that you have the right people in place. To project based on marketing, you need to know your average case value and the average length of a matter. And then you do a little math.

If your average case value is $60,000 and the average case length is six months, then you know each matter will bill an average of $10,000 a month, for six months, before it closes. By deciding how many cases you are going to open each month, your revenue will fall into a natural pattern. This method is great if you are starting a new marketing initiative or if you are continuing one where you know exactly what will happen.

This is the case for an estate planning attorney in Dallas with whom we worked. Every time Whit[60] gave a speech, he would get three new clients. Each client is worth $5,000 that pays in that month. For planning purposes, we coordinated Whit's speaking schedule to project his revenue. All we had to do was project the number of speeches in a month and add $15,000 to that month's revenue stream (3 clients at $5K each). It's not always so straightforward. The downloadable billing grid mentioned has a tab set up to project revenues by case acquisition, so feel free to download and use it.

The billing grid also includes a case acquisition tab with six different types of cases listed. The types of cases handled by your firm can impact profitability. Understanding which cases cost more to handle and which generate more profit may encourage you to change the balance of your case mix.

The case acquisition tab provides insight into this process and ensures that you project and record your revenues by case type. This is especially important for flat-fee firms, but hourly firms also need to take this step. As you grow, you will notice that different types of cases put different stresses on the resources of your firm. You might realize that certain matters take more paralegal time, and others are more attorney intensive.

Those differences influence your bottom line. The ability to track revenue and change your marketing focus to achieve a more profitable case mix is a powerful tool. You might as well start doing this now— the smaller your firm, the easier it is to implement.

We usually say a firm should handle four to six different areas (or types of cases) within their practice. Six is the absolute limit. Just to clarify, when I say different areas of their practice, I mean different case

---

[60]   Whit is my uncle's name. Actually, it's Whitney and his son, daughter, and my sister were all named after him. Mostly middle names.

types. For example, a family law firm specializes in one primary area of practice, but coordinates numerous case types within that focus, such as divorce with children, divorce without children, modifications, and adoptions.

Either by using a traditional billing grid or by projecting based on case acquisitions, you should have a revenue number. Now, we need to do a reasonability test. Is your revenue number reasonable? If you did $250,000 last year, and you are planning on $5 million this year, I am going to have to say the number does not pass the sniff test. Try again.

Are you projecting revenue that is double what you did this year? That might be fine if you know you have a marketing plan to ramp up sales, the ability to hire the people you need, and you have a history of big growth. We would rather be more conservative with revenue numbers—it is just the safest, most prudent route. This is the hardest step in the Profit Planning process, but at this point, you should have revenue numbers for each month.

Step 2: Expenses

Okay, are you still with me? We are about 40 percent of the way through the Profit Planning process. Hopefully, this has not been too painful so far. And hopefully, you have done some dreaming about what you really want this coming year. Remember, you are telling yourself, your team, your family, and possibly your banker, what your plan is for the coming year. Make sure it is what you want. Now comes the second and easiest part of the whole process: figuring out current expenses. Again, we have a few methods, but the one we like the best is still to write a story and then put some numbers next to it.

Pull out your profit and loss (P&L) sheet from the last four to six months and write down how you spent your money in each category. Start with your people—who is on payroll, and what salary do you pay them? Add that up, and you have your payroll number. Don't forget to put yourself in there. You provide a great service to your firm, and if you weren't there, you would have to hire somebody to replace you. For your salary, you should be getting the amount you would have to pay someone else to do your job.[61] Below that, multiply payroll by the percent you pay in federal and state taxes and add that. If you have benefits, such as health insurance or a 401K, write that down and then put in some numbers.

Next up are your overhead numbers. Start with a line for your rent then add office expenses, like copier rental costs, the monthly lease payment, your office phone (and probably your cell phone), and any other expenses you can find. A great place to check to make sure you have included all of your expenses is to go to your Cash Flow Forecast and see what is on there. Add every single recurring bill to your expense list and make sure that you are doing this for each month.

Once the recurring expenses are in, refer back to your P&L and see if there are any one-off expenses you need to add. Bar dues are the first that come to mind. Those are usually paid once a year. And what about end-of-year bonuses? Don't forget those. Your firm can't be profitable without a happy team. Once you have written down all the expenses, start projecting them out over each month. For months that have a one-time expense (like Bar dues), make a note, so you remember why it is different.

Now you have a basic budget. This is what most accountants would suggest. And it looks an awful lot like what you did last year. That's not what we want from a Profit Plan. The next step makes it a Profit Plan.

Step 3: Dream

It is time to dream again. What direction do you want to go? What changes or investments do you want to make? Do you want to move to a new space? If so, when? How much do you think it is going to cost? Any landlord will want first month's rent, last month's rent, and a deposit. You will probably also have some buildout costs. Put those in there. Oh, and don't forget the movers.

---

[61] And remember that the IRS requires you to have a "reasonable" salary. Still wish they would better define reasonable …

Have you been talking to somebody about a great new online marketing agency that has been working for them? Do you want to try that? That's great, but do you have a new marketing plan that goes along with it? One of my biggest pet peeves is when attorneys come to me and say, "I need $10,000 a month for marketing." My response is always, "What are you going to do with the money, and what are the anticipated results?" The response I usually get is, "I'm not sure. But I know that if I spend the money, I'll get more clients."

That is not a marketing plan—that is a hope and a prayer. And we don't believe in the hope and pray method of marketing. You should know that if you spend a certain amount of money, within a specific amount of time, you should be seeing a minimum number of new clients. If you don't have a plan like this, you can get sucked into big expenses that have no ROI (Return on Investment).

A good marketing plan will not only have a strategy for increasing revenue, but it will also include measurable goals, which are a safety net for you. Remember Walter's story about the TV ads? Marketing plans help you know when something is not working so you can stop. There is no reason to keep throwing good money after bad. Move on to something that will give you a better ROI. A marketing plan can also allow you to do things you never thought possible. Because it lays out what you expect to happen, it gives you the confidence to try new things.

Dreaming is fun and can be very profitable for your firm. At this point in the process, you should be chomping at the bit for the new year so you can finally have the firm of your dreams (literally). Put those dreams into your plan.

Step 4: Bottom Line

Now that you have gathered all your basic revenue and expense information and have layered on your dreams, let's look at the fourth step, the bottom line, or what I like to call profit. Are you getting a

30 percent profit margin each month? Some months will naturally be higher and some lower, but at year-end, are you *at least* getting 20 percent? If you are not, then at this point, you really need to review the billing grid. Did you plan a new marketing activity to start in July that should have a corresponding bump in revenue? And do you have enough people to work all those new cases?

Go back and compare revenue to marketing, to people, and to other expenses. You will find that one addition or change means a bunch of other things need to be tweaked. For example, when you hire a new staff member, revenue needs to be increased, as does your case management software subscription and possibly your phone (if you need to add an extension). Additionally, bar dues will rise, malpractice insurance changes at renewal, and you might want to bump up your office supplies a little. Don't get overwhelmed. Just think about the way your firm is interconnected and make the adjustments. Think through the story.

Now, how does your profit look? Is it better? Is it worse? If you aren't hitting the amount of profit you want, start looking at your expenses. Are they all necessary? The first place I always look is marketing because until your firm hits about $750,000 a year in revenue, the vast majority of clients come from client referrals, professional referrals, and networking—basically from your reputation. And those are "free" except for your networking time. Go back and make more adjustments. Remember, the point of this exercise is more profit, which means more money in your pocket.

Now is a good time to revisit the Rule of Thirds—one-third to people, one-third to overhead, and one-third to profit. Are you hitting those basic ratios? Then get a little more granular on that subject. Refer back to the Profit Finder grid in the Ideal Ratios chapter. Granular answers are exactly what you get from it. It tells you where you are overspending and underspending, and by how much. Using this, you know specifically what parts of your Profit Plan need adjustment to hit ideal ratios.

Another way to look at this is to download Cathedral Capital's Profit Finder spreadsheet at CathCap.com/PanictoProfitResources.

Following the directions on the spreadsheet, put in your year-end revenue numbers, your salary, your total payroll numbers (including you), your planned marketing expenses, and your overhead numbers. Where are you out of kilter?

I know that at this point, many of you are tired, frustrated, and wondering why you are spending the time. Just remember the popular saying, "Failing to plan is planning to fail." And you are almost finished—this is your last set of revisions. So, take one more look, make a few adjustments, and put it back in the Profit Finder to make sure you are pretty close to where you want to be. Then, send the whole thing to your bookkeeper to put in QuickBooks. Whew, your Profit Plan is done! And you have a plan for the coming year.

Remember, this is the document that you use to keep you on track—to make adjustments throughout the year to ensure you hit your goals. While it might take a couple of hours to organize, isn't getting a profitable firm worth it?

Results

After doing all of this work to create a profit plan, it may feel like you should be set for the year, but every small business owner knows that you're never done! Profit plans are only as relevant as the information they contain. Every day brings new challenges and developments, so it is essential that you review and update your profit plan on a monthly basis (or more frequently if things change).

I was working with a wonderful family law attorney named Win[62] who has a profitable and very fast-growing law firm. As of this

---

62   Win is a cousin who is probably the most humble, sweetest, caring guy ever born. His wife, whom he started dating in seventh or eighth grade is equally as sweet. What's truly amazing is that he has had an incredible career in the oil and gas industry and done amazing things, yet he is the same sweet Win he was back when he was 20. None of his success has gone to his head. He also has this thing about his socks. He believes when you buy them as a pair they must remain in that same exact pair. His mother finally made him pin his socks together before putting them in the laundry so they wouldn't ever get separated. His wife was happy to inherit that process.

printing, he has made the Inc. 5000 list three times. The list identifies the country's top 5,000 fastest growing companies, and I know he will hit it again this year. When it came time to do his profit planning, Win could tell me exactly where he wanted to go. It was our job, using his Profit Plan, to help develop the roadmap to get there, and we did. It was a thing of beauty.

He promptly used information from the Profit Plan to secure a loan to cover his plans. Because fast-growing law firms like his are complete cash monsters, sometimes it feels like there is not enough cash to feed the beast. With the line of credit Win got, we were able to make all his plans for the year come true. He moved offices, hired new staff, and launched new marketing campaigns.

But these changes didn't happen on the schedule we had devised. Within the first three months of the year, we realized our timeline was wrong. He was moving much faster than we had anticipated, so we needed to revise the Profit Plan—like now! This is really common. At the end of the day, every profit plan is nothing more than an assortment of educated guesses. For this reason, it needs to be looked at and adjusted on a regular basis, sometimes monthly.

Your profit plan is a living, breathing document that changes with your firm. What should you do when you land a big case, have the perfect paralegal show up on your doorstep, or your building gets bought, and you have three months to move? You need to adjust. The more information you have and put into your Profit Plan, the more accurate it will be.

Profit Plans Are for More Than Your Own Planning

A couple of years ago, when Win's firm was growing really fast, he needed a line of credit to be able to keep up with the growth. We worked together and prepared a really good loan package. The firm was profitable (though he was reinvesting a lot of the profit back into the firm).

He wasn't taking an unseemly amount of cash out, and we had a great narrative about why he needed the loan, how it would be used, and how it would contribute to future profit. Once he was well prepped, I sent him off to the bank. He returned completely undone. The conversation went something like this:

Win: I'm never going to get this loan. The whole firm is going to implode because of stupid bankers.

Me: Win, what happened?

Win: Seriously? They want completely unrealistic things.

Me: Win, what did they say?

Win: They want Pro Formas! My whole firm is going to crater because I don't have some stupid report they want.

Me: Win, you know that Profit Plan (Budget) we put together?

Win: Yes

Me: That's a Pro Forma.

Win: (extended silence) Are you kidding me? They put me through all of this, and they just wanted to see my budget? (Getting louder). Why didn't they just say that? Cuss Word ... Cuss Word ... Name Calling (none of which is like Win, AT ALL).

Had I not been there to talk Win through what the bank was saying, he would have abandoned his attempt to get a line of credit, and he probably would not have made the Inc. 5000 list for the past three years.

The point of the story is that Profit Plans are used by people outside your firm too.

ABOUT THE AUTHOR

Brooke Lively is the CEO and founder of Cathedral Capital, a consortium of CFOs and profitability strategists committed to equipping entrepreneurial law firm owners with the critical tools and expertise to take their businesses to the next level.

Brooke's mission is to make meaningful connections with her clients, helping them design and realize their unique vision of success. Leading with her competencies in financial expertise and executive coaching, Brooke thrives on nurturing her clients' growth—whether that's growth measured by the bottom line or by their impact in their respective communities and industries.

"I'm passionate about numbers. I'm passionate about building leaders. And I'm passionate about finding where these intersect for entrepreneurs and law firm owners. My greatest joy comes from walking alongside my clients—helping them chart their course, overcome obstacles, discover their hidden strengths, and scale the peaks they never imagined they could conquer."

Empowering clients with her signature frameworks and tools, and arming them with her financial insights and strategies, Brooke elevates leaders' efficacy and influence, and helps take their businesses to new heights of sustainable profitability.

Brooke was recognized by the *Fort Worth Business Press* as one of "Fort Worth's 2016 CFOs of the Year," *Diversity Journal* listed her as one of its "Women Worth Watching" for the past four years, and the *Better Business Bureau of Fort Worth* named her to their inaugural "Top 25

Women to Watch." She teaches CLE for various Bar Associations and is a highly rated speaker with organizations such as Entrepreneur's Organization, Wealth Counsel, and Bay Area Legal Incubator.

With over ten years of experience in the financial services industry, Brooke received her MBA in investments and corporate finance from Texas Christian University in Fort Worth, Texas. She also earned the prestigious and globally recognized Chartered Financial Analyst designation, the highest level of credentials in the global investment management industry.

Brooke works with clients across the nation and has a voracious appetite for travel, but most enjoys spending time with her dog, Katie, at their home in Fort Worth, Texas.

CPSIA information can be obtained
at www.ICGtesting.com
Printed in the USA
LVHW050913191121
703659LV00003B/6/J